LIFE AND CONSCIOUSNESS

Life and Consciousness
J. R. Ench

Publisher: Life Engineering Foundation,
Delta Avenue, Bridgewater, Iowa, USA, 50837-8015

Editor: Life Engineering Foundation,
Calgary Centre, Alberta, Canada

Literary Consultant: Johanna M. Bates, Literary Consultants Inc,
Calgary, Alberta, Canada

Book Design: ThinkDesign Ltd., Calgary, Alberta, Canada

Printing: AGMV Marquis Imprimeur Inc.

**To order JREnch Books by credit card, call toll free:
1-800-421-2667 (US & Canada). Ask for department 100.
To fax your order: 1-712-779-2095. Include credit card information.
Mail: JREnch Books, Dept. 100, 109 Main Street, Massena, Iowa, 50853, USA
E-Mail: jrenchbooks@lifeengineering.org
Website: http://www.lifeengineering.org/book**

ISBN: 0-9672814-0-7

Printed in Canada

Dedicated to: Dr. Thurman Fleet

Dr. Fleet devoted his life to assisting his fellow man in breaking the chains that have enslaved him physically, mentally and spiritually.

EDITOR'S NOTE

What you are about to read has been compiled by a group who offers it to you in oneness. The information contained within this book is a correlation of knowledge of the physical, mental and spiritual worlds, and at times, it may conflict with your own accepted ideas. Many references are made that correlate modern science with the major religions of the world. If your understanding of life is not based upon a correlation of the two, you have a limited view of life.

We ask you to neither accept nor reject the information in this book until you have had time to think about it and do some investigating on your own. While reading this book, do not allow what you have been taught or what you have previously accepted to interfere with the information being presented. This will give you the freedom to analyze the material without bias. One of man's greatest shortcomings is his tendency to jump to conclusions without knowing the facts.

The book *Life and Consciousness* was written by Dr. J.R. Ench and was first published in 1980. We hope that this new revised edition will give the words even more life and bring greater consciousness to its readers.

LIFE
& CONSCIOUSNESS

by J. R. Ench

TABLE OF CONTENTS

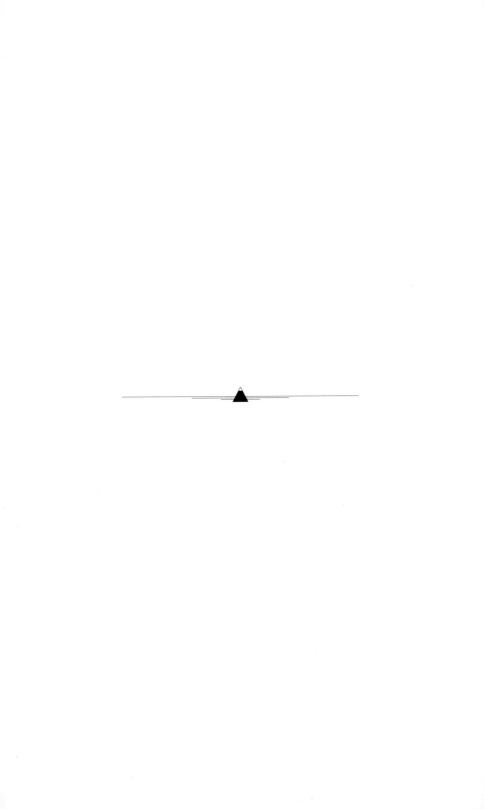

What Is life?

What is 'life'? Seeking the answer to this question became a lifelong quest of Robert Casper, the main character of this story. Webster's Standard Collegiate Dictionary defines *Life* in four ways:

Life: The vital force, whether regarded as physical or spiritual, the presence of which distinguishes organic from inorganic matter.

Life: The quality or character distinguishing an animal or a plant from inorganic or from dead organic bodies.

Life: The series of experiences, of body and mind, which make up the history of an animal or human from birth to death.

Life: Existence, especially conscious existence, conceived as a quality of the soul or as the soul's nature and being.

Down through the ages, mankind has accepted certain personalities as being 'the authorities', without questioning the accuracy of the knowledge they imparted. For instance, the Greek philosopher Aristotle was accepted as the authority of his day concerning the nature of things. Even after Galileo had tested and disproved Aristotle's theories, the Church as the supreme authority forced Galileo to recant his findings or face excommunication and possibly execution. In 1628, an English physician by the name of William Harvey published his book, *Motus Cordis,* in which he advanced the new idea that the blood circulated through the body, rather than ebbing and flowing like the tides. Just as Galileo faced ridicule by critics of his day, many so-called seventeenth century scholars scoffed at Harvey's new ideas. In like manner, the English chemist Joseph Priestly, who discovered the element oxygen, did not accept the principles of combustion proven by Antoine Lavoisier. Priestly, to his dying day, adhered to the illogical Phlogiston theory, which assumed the existence of an unproven substance contained in all combustible matter.

Any new discovery, idea, observation or invention faces resistance and even ridicule by the conventional opinion of its day before it is finally accepted. This has been proven time and time again. We know that man with his limited, acquired beliefs did not readily accept Robert Fulton and his steamboat, Alexander Graham Bell and his telephone, the Wright Brothers and their airplane, or Thomas Edison and the electric light bulb. We can be thankful that from time to time some daring individuals have appeared upon the stage of life and have challenged conventional opinion. If not for these individuals, we would still be living in the dark ages.

The findings of Sir Isaac Newton, an English physicist, are referred to today as classical physics. The principles he discovered were the basis of all physics up until the beginning of the twentieth century. Until recently, all research by physicists was based upon the application of these principles.

In order to explain the propagation of light through space in terms of classical physics, a medium was required; scientists called this medium *ether*. In 1887, Albert Michelson and Edward Morley conducted an experiment to either prove or disprove the existence of this medium. The result of the experiment indicated that the ether did not exist. The conclusion was that classical physics could not explain the propagation of light through space. This was a shattering turn of events in the scientific community. In the years following, George Fitzgerald and Hendrik Lorentz developed mathematical formulae that offered a new interpretation to the results obtained by the Michelson-Morley experiment. Their alternate theory proposed that the measurements in the experiment could have been inaccurate due to the relative nature of time and space. Because they could not think beyond the framework of classical physics, all these scientists were limited by their fixed beliefs. Even today, high school and university students are still being indoctrinated with these limited beliefs.

At the beginning of the twentieth century, there appeared upon the scene a twenty-six year old man whose consciousness had not been colored by these established beliefs of science. Unaffected by the restrictions of classical physics, he was truly free to think upon the phenomena of light and other forces of nature. He promulgated new conclusions to solve the unanswered scientific problems of his time. Although most scientists rejected his ideas, these new ideas influenced a few thinkers to study them, make observations, and finally prove them to be correct. This man, Albert Einstein, is recognized today as the father of modern physics. His theory of relativity enables us to free ourselves from enslavement to fixed and limiting beliefs. Today, in philosophy, education and even theology, more and more of the limiting, accepted beliefs are being questioned and cast aside.

As this story unfolds, you will learn that Robert Casper, from an early age, had the same questioning nature as those who have been mentioned above. He eventually began seeking answers to four basic questions:

WHO AM I?

FROM
WHERE HAVE I COME?

WHAT IS
MY PURPOSE FOR EXISTING?

WHAT IS
MY GOAL AND DESTINY?

Knowingly or unknowingly, all of us have asked ourselves these questions at one time or another. Reasoning upon these questions concerning life, Robert Casper knew there had to be an answer to them all, and so he began his quest.

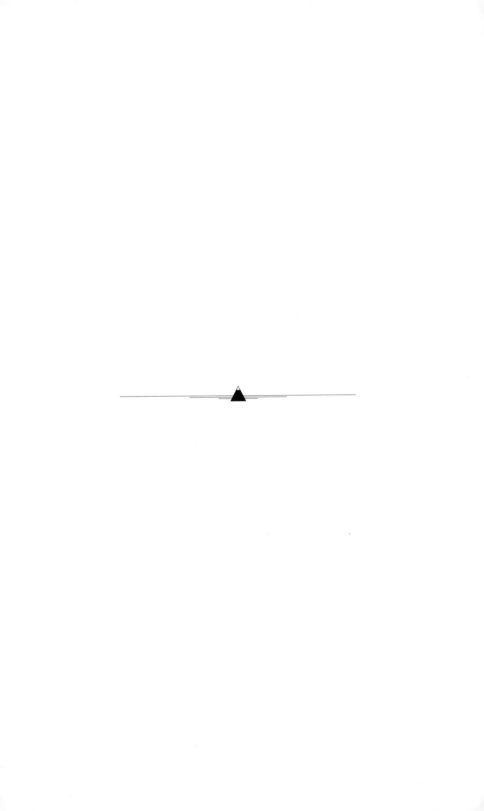

PART I

Who Am I?

WHO AM I?

It was a cold, wintry November day. In a matter of minutes the sirens would go off, breaking the stillness, making everyone aware that it was eleven a.m. The sirens signified the third anniversary of the ending of the First World War, "a war to make the world forever safe for democracy". Downstairs, in his large two-story house, Bill Casper paced the floor. He was waiting for the nurse to come hurrying down the stairs, hoping she would announce that he was the father of a fine baby boy.

Teresa, a small four-year-old child, was sitting on the couch, watching her daddy pace back and forth. She had been told that this very day she would have a new baby brother. From a room upstairs there could occasionally be heard a low, painful moan or a loud cry of anguish. Suddenly, the moans and cries were drowned out by the shrill noise of the town sirens. At the exact moment the sirens ceased their noise, Dr. Phillips delivered the baby!

It was customary to observe five minutes of silence after the sirens had ceased, and so a complete hush came over the Casper household. During the silence however, Dr. Phillips worked frantically! The baby's face was covered with a thin film of tissue. After an eternity of minutes, Dr. Phillips had carefully removed the tissue from around the baby's face so that the baby could then get air into its lungs. He promptly picked the baby up by its feet and gave it a hardy smack on its backside. Still, there was no sound. He kept slapping and slapping and was just about to accept the possibility that the infant was dead. Then suddenly, a good healthy cry gushed forth from the baby's little body. Exactly five minutes of silence commemorating Armistice Day had been observed by everyone in the Casper household.

One week later, the baby was christened into the Catholic faith and was given the name Robert Joseph. As was the custom, many relatives and friends attended the christening. When they were told of the baby's unusual condition at birth murmurs spread through the group. This unusual condition was very rare indeed! They declared it a good omen and all went home saying that this child, born with a 'veil', would someday possess a rare and wonderful gift.

At the age of five, Robert was showing the normal behavioral patterns of most other five-year-olds, with one exception. Robert Casper had an insatiable curiosity! We all know that most little boys have an affinity for bugs and other creeping things. In general they will watch them, poke them and be a nuisance to the poor things. Mercifully for bugs, a small boy's attention span is very short. Before long he is off doing something else that has drawn his attention. This was not the case with Robert. He was not easily satisfied and he would often enlist the help of older family members to capture and place bugs in jars. This allowed him to watch their antics by the hour.

Books also captured Robert's attention. He loved to have someone read to him and show him pictures in his storybooks. He also loved turning the pages of his father's National Geographic magazines, even though he was constantly scolded for taking them from the family bookcases.

Late one summer afternoon, Robert was playing with a boat that he had made out of an old piece of wood and a fistful of rusty nails. At the same time, his father was watering the grass out front, causing a stream to form alongside the curbstone. Robert was sailing his boat in the stream and watching his father when all of a sudden he stood up, ran over and asked, "Daddy, where did the grass come from? Why don't it grow on the sidewalk?" Bill Casper was amazed and it dawned on him just how acutely observant Robert was of all his surroundings. After quietly reflecting for a moment, Bill started to explain, in the simplest terms possible, how grass grows out of the ground from seeds. He explained that unless seeds fall on soft dirt, they couldn't sprout and produce grass. "But Daddy," queried Robert, "where do the seeds come from?"

Trying to find a way out of what could have been a long question-and-answer predicament, Bill summed it up with, "Son, you and everything you see around you were created by God." Robert never forgot how this answer puzzled him and how it raised within him another question that, to this day, remains unanswered. **Who is God?**

Some years later, after reading his little green Catechism, Robert had his next 'encounter' with God. Robert pondered on the following questions and answers from his Catechism: "Who is God? ...God is the Creator of heaven and earth and all things"; "Where is God? ...God is everywhere"; "Did God have a beginning? ...God had no beginning, nor does He have an end."

Because Robert was born into a 'good Catholic family', he was sent to parochial school. There he was taught that God consists of three parts: God the Father, God the Son and God the Holy Spirit. Each morning before the first class, and each afternoon before dismissal, the children were required to say their prayers. The prayers began by making the sign of the cross. This was done by first touching their foreheads, their chests, and finally their left and right shoulders, while at the same time repeating the words, "In the name of the Father, the Son and the Holy Spirit, Amen."

What did these words mean? Robert didn't have the faintest idea and he assumed that none of his classmates knew either. Although most of the children just accepted these things without question, this was not so with Robert! Something within him compelled him to want to know the significance of making the sign of the cross and saying the prayer. He wanted to know the meaning and significance of all the things he was learning in Catechism and Sunday Mass. In sixth grade, he became an altar boy and began studying his Catechism earnestly. From this time on, Robert's thoughts concerning God and creation became his greatest concern.

His first attempt to visualize God creating a man reminded him of his younger days, when he used to make mud pies. He visualized God as a man, molding clay with his hands, forming a body. Robert could also imagine God breathing 'the breath of life' into man. He had heard about the biblical account of man's creation in which God had formed man out of the dust of the ground, and so his mental picture of creation seemed logical to his young mind. Robert had also heard that man was made 'in the image and likeness of God', and so he reasoned that if God could make things, he was also a creator.

One thing continued to puzzle Robert. If God could make man out of the dust of the ground, why did He have to take a rib out of man to make woman? Why couldn't He have also created the woman out of the dust? Throughout high school and his first year of college, these kinds of questions concerning creation continued to occupy Robert's consciousness. As he continued to advance in his education, his acceptance of the *Genesis* story broke down completely. This was due not only to his study of science, but also to the contradictions he discovered from his continued study of the biblical account of creation.

While Robert was attending parochial school, Jesus became his hero. He felt in his heart and mind that whatever Jesus had spoken was the truth. As he grew older, Robert resolved to live the teachings of Jesus to the best of his ability, even though he could not fully understand the meaning of some of the statements. Upon questioning those who taught and preached Jesus' message, Robert discovered that they did not know the meanings either, because they could not answer his questions. Robert was seeking the truth because his hero had said, "Know the truth and the truth shall make you free."

Years later, after having been educated in science and having put his education to practical use, Robert reasoned that if all the knowledge of science was true, and if all the teachings in the Holy Scriptures were true, then science and religion had to be true together. Robert wondered if it was just a matter of misinterpretation that made theology appear contradictory to science. If so, could science and theology be reconciled? Was this possible? Could there be another interpretation of the biblical story of creation? Robert resolved to know the answers.

AM I A BODY?

Because he was a Catholic, Robert had never read the Bible. His only knowledge of the Scriptures was from selected parts that were read by the priest each Sunday at Mass. Robert realized that if he were to follow the teaching of Jesus, "Know the truth and the truth shall make you free", he would need to review all the knowledge he had ever gained from his schooling and from his religion. This included reading the Bible for the first time.

He began reviewing his knowledge by asking himself several questions. Where shall I begin? What shall I investigate first? More than anything else, I am conscious of my own physical existence. I see, hear and feel. I am conscious of being alive, but really, who am I? Am I a body? This last question struck a chord within Robert. He decided that this last question was the only place to begin, to find out who or what he really was. The decision of where to start was settled, and Robert was then free to pursue this subject. Knowing that either he was the body or had a body, Robert wanted to know its composition.

It is common knowledge that the body comes into existence due to the fusion of two nearly microscopic units. One unit, the ovum, is so small in size that twelve of them can fit on the head of a pin. The other unit, the sperm, is even smaller. It requires approximately two hundred sperm to cover the ovum. Therefore, it would seem that our bodies do materialize from 'grains of dust'.

Wanting to know the composition of the sperm and ovum and knowing that they were matter, Robert recalled the first chapter in his high school chemistry book, "What Is Matter?" In reviewing this chapter, he searched for the most elementary composition of the body. These 'grains of dust' had been found to consist of six separate, distinct, smaller units called *elements*. These elements were hydrogen, carbon, nitrogen, oxygen, phosphorous and sulfur. Chemistry proved that these elements were the basic building blocks of the human body. Robert came to realize the truth in the statement, "The Lord God formed man of the dust of the ground."

The science of chemistry had its origin in the ages long past. Perhaps its beginning was the very moment that early man stooped down, swept up a stone from the ground and questioned its composition. Where did it come from? How was it created? Robert reasoned that the writer of the *Genesis* account of creation might have exhibited this same type of curiosity. The writer may have asked these same types of questions. One question in particular might have been, "Where did heaven and earth come from?" Perhaps a clear sky was observed and a cloud was seen to form out of what appeared to be nothingness. Then the wind blew, other clouds gathered and the sky became dark. Perhaps with the darkness came a flash of lightning, then the roar of thunder, and finally the fall of rain. This manifestation of rain, coming from out of 'nothingness', may have led the writer of *Genesis* to conclude that heaven and earth could have been fashioned in a similar manner. However speculative this analogy, it nevertheless gave Robert a new insight into the written account of creation. *Genesis* states that, "...the earth was without form". Robert concluded, that "earth" did not refer to planet Earth, but rather to the 'stuff' of which all matter is made.

Man's attempt to further understand matter led him to study its properties and the forces that affect it. Early investigators concluded that everything was composed of only four things: earth, air, fire and water. This classification of matter, originated by ancient Greek philosophers, was commonly accepted by the masses. However, a few thinkers came along who started to question and investigate this belief.

Democritus, an ancient Greek philosopher, postulated that as matter is broken down into smaller and smaller units, there must ultimately be a unit that can no longer be divided. He called this indivisible unit an *atom*. His hypothesis was not accepted by the foremost authorities of his day nor was it later accepted by Plato or Aristotle. However, man eventually began to break down and further investigate all matter. In so doing, he ultimately discovered that everything, inanimate or animate, was made up of ninety-two units of matter called elements. With this knowledge, scientists then discovered that the human body was composed of the six primary elements previously mentioned. "From dust thou art," claimed the Bible. "From dust thou art," science had no doubt.

After investigating matter, science turned its attention to the forces that affect matter. Early man lived in fear of the destructive force of lightning and he bowed down before it in order to appease it. For ages, man continued to be afraid of this phenomenon. It wasn't until the eighteenth century that a great American statesman, Benjamin Franklin, dared to investigate it. In order to do so, he sent a kite into the sky during a storm to try and capture the force of lightning. Having captured some of this force, Franklin was amazed to discover that it was just a great electric charge. The charge was similar to an electric spark that investigators produced by rubbing certain substances together. By this time, these investigators were becoming known as scientists, and each of their fields of study became an individual branch of science.

Scientists began to discover means of producing the force they now call electricity. They also discovered ways to store this electricity for later use. They soon found that certain combinations of elements would also release this force. Next, they found a mechanical means of generating large quantities of electricity. Finally, with controlled use of this energy, man was able to light up the world and dispel the darkness.

Science later discovered that some of the elements gave off a form of radiation from within themselves. Antoine-Henri Becquerel, a French physicist and the discoverer of uranium, accidentally placed a piece of pitchblende in a drawer alongside an unexposed photographic plate. Later, when he removed the plate from the drawer, he discovered that it had been exposed to some form of radiation. He concluded that the radiation must have come from the ore that was accidentally placed alongside the photographic plate.

Madame Curie, a Polish chemist and an associate of Becquerel, was immediately informed of his accidental discovery. She then began to investigate the properties of the ore. After many years of research, Curie isolated the element radium from the ore. She discovered that, in its pure state, this new element had three distinct emanations: alpha rays, beta rays and gamma rays. This discovery initiated a whole new branch of study.

At about the same time, William Crookes invented a specialized glass tube called a cathode ray tube. By utilizing and improving this tube, Joseph John Thomson discovered that beta rays were negatively charged particles. He also discovered that these particles were found within the atom and in electric currents. He named these particles *electrons*.

Lord Rutherford also investigated radium rays and discovered that alpha rays were the nuclei of helium atoms, which possessed a positive charge. Further research led him to discover that all atoms had similar, massive centers. He called this massive center the nucleus. Rutherford discovered that inside the nuclei were smaller, positively charged units of mass. He named these units *protons*.

These discoveries proved that the atom was not an indivisible unit, but that it consisted of subatomic particles. Rutherford's model of the atom was analogous to a small solar system. The nucleus represented the central sun and the electrons, whirling around the nucleus, represented the planets. Each atom was composed of a different number and arrangement of electrons and each contained a nucleus. Rutherford's model of the atom enabled scientists to describe and account for the differences between the ninety-two elements.

While researching the structure of the nucleus, scientists discovered that the atomic number was, with the exception of hydrogen, always less than the atomic mass. This created another problem; something was wrong with Rutherford's model. In 1932, James Chadwick discovered a neutrally charged particle located in the nucleus that was later named the *neutron*. This discovery accounted for the measured differences between the atomic number and the mass of the atoms. In 1935, Chadwick was awarded the Nobel Prize in Physics for his discovery of the neutron.

Due to the long, hard and tedious efforts of a few, it has been ascertained that each atom has at its center a nucleus that contains protons and neutrons, and orbiting around the nucleus are the electrons. It has further been proven that it is the number, arrangement and distribution of the electrons that draw atoms together to form the elements, then the molecules, and finally, every physical thing that exists.

Having researched all this knowledge on the discovery of the composition of matter, it then became clear to Robert that his ultimate, physical beginning was from the arrangement of positively, negatively and neutrally charged particles. It was not from the uniting of the sperm and the ovum, as he had previously thought.

In August of 1945, World War II suddenly ended. The United States dropped atomic bombs on Hiroshima and Nagasaki. A tremendous force was released from within the nucleus of atoms, causing destruction, the likes of which had never before been seen. Since this awesome event, a whole new field of investigation called *nuclear physics* has evolved. Scientists have discovered that by changing the structure of the nucleus, new elements can be formed and one element can be transformed into another. As a result of this knowledge, scientists have since discovered that our sun and stars furnish us with heat and light due to the transformation of hydrogen into helium. This transformation process is called *fusion*. Hydrogen, the simplest of all elements, contains only one proton and one electron. Within the stars, hydrogen is the basic building block from which all other elements are formed.

At this point in his research, Robert began to feel that he had some information with which to work. It was then logical to him that these latest findings could be correlated with *The Book of Genesis*. *Genesis* implied that, at first, God alone existed in space or in the void.

> *In the beginning God created the heaven and the earth. And the earth was without form, and void; and darkness was upon the face of the deep. And the Spirit of God moved upon the face of the waters. And God said, Let there be light: and there was light.*

Recent research has led to the discovery of other subatomic units with the same mass as the electron but with an opposite charge. These subatomic units are called positrons or positive electrons. If an electron collides with a positron, they annihilate each other. In the process, a massive amount of energy is released in the form of photons of light. Robert thought that this discovery could explain the biblical account of the first day of creation. It had to! It was the only logical answer.

Science has proven that all matter in the entire universe is composed of one essential essence. They call this essence *energy*. Science does not know what it is nor from where it came, but it does know that it is everywhere. Similarly, theology teaches us that God is the essential essence, that God is unknown and that He is all that exists. Just as science cannot know what energy is, the Scriptures inform us that the finite mind of man can never know God, the infinite.

Could God and energy be one and the same? Robert contemplated this concept for a long time. Going back over his Catechism, he pondered on the answer to the question,

has no end. Eastern religions also look upon
having created the universe. The expansion
is referred to by eastern religions as *cosmic*
this first cause will eventually draw the
into itself. This contraction is called *cosmic*
eligions state that this cycle of cosmic day and
repeated eternally.

lain where the original mass of the Big Bang
some scientists postulated a third theory.
as known as the *oscillating theory* of the uni-
l that as the effect of the Big Bang explosion
everything in the universe will finally come to
if all the mass in the universe is great enough,
forces between bodies will cause them all to
ether, forming another cosmic egg. This cosmic
en explode again, creating a perpetual cycle of
aths of the universe. Today however, scientists
timates of all mass in the universe and do not
ere is a sufficient amount to cause the universe
nd thus, substantiate the oscillating theory.

over his research and reviewing it over and
Robert became totally amazed to learn how
Genesis story of creation really was. As the
his discovery enveloped him, he began to
sing prayer he had often repeated in church;
the beginning, is now, ever shall be, world
Amen." Remembering this prayer, something
vithin him. Robert knew that he was *not* a
ence, matter did not exist. Matter was only an
, of units or quanta of the unknown. Whether
n was God or whether it was energy, Robert
e was of *it*, but was definitely not a body.

"Where is God?" The answer in the Catechism had stated, "God is everywhere." Science knows that the entire physical universe is composed of nothing but matter and energy. Furthermore, science has proven that matter is just another form of energy. From this, Robert concluded that if God is everywhere and energy is everywhere, then the two have to be synonymous. They must be, without a doubt, one and the same.

Next, Robert started to review what he had been taught about thermodynamics. The first law of thermodynamics stated that energy can neither be created nor destroyed; it always has and always will exist. Because Robert knew that God and energy were synonymous, he realized that he could then comprehend the answer to another question in his Catechism, "Did God have a beginning?" From this, Robert could scientifically accept the first verse in *The Book of Genesis*. God, or energy, had no beginning and existed in the void before creation.

Creation began when this unknown essence sent forth units of itself and created a high and low potential of energy. Robert knew that whenever there was a difference in potential, energy flowed from the high to the low potential. Science called this flow *kinetic energy*, and theology called it *Spirit*. Robert reasoned that it could be called either kinetic energy or Spirit, but when it affected matter, the expression of the matter was called its life. Could this moving energy have been the first cause of light in the universe? Robert knew from science that when electrons and positrons collided and annihilated each other, photons of light were released from the explosion. In the beginning, there must have been nothing but light, electromagnetic radiation.

Robert had learned that for many years, science did not have a satisfactory theory concerning the origin of the universe. However, there were many theories concerning the nature of the universe and one theory was Hoyle's *steady state theory*. In essence, this theory simply stated that hydrogen was constantly being created in the universe in order to replace matter that was being destroyed. His theory was in opposition to the first law of thermodynamics. Hoyle theorized that hydrogen was destroyed inside the thermonuclear reactions in the stars. A few scientists, however, continued to observe the starry sky in order to obtain more information concerning creation, which would either prove or disprove Hoyle's theory. It was later discovered that, in these thermonuclear processes, hydrogen was being converted into helium. During this conversion, four hydrogen atoms fused together, forming one helium atom. In this process, the difference in the mass between four hydrogen atoms and one helium atom was converted directly into radiant energy. This was why the stars shined. The quantity of radiant energy that was released could be calculated by applying Albert Einstein's famous formula, $E=mc^2$. This formula stated that energy (E) was equal to the mass (m) times the speed of light (c) squared.

Edwin Hubble, an American astronomer, and his co-worker, Milton Humason, were able to determine that science had drastically underestimated the number of stars in the universe. While studying what they thought were gas nebulae, they discovered that these gas clouds were, in fact, clusters of stars. They were credited with naming these star clusters *galaxies*. After calculating their speed and studying the spectrum of light emanating from them, these men determined that the galaxies were all rushing away from one another. They concluded that at one time all of these galaxies must

have been closer tog
galaxies were all rushi
dous speed, these men
have been a terrific
observations led to a n
universe. This theory b

All explosions consist
energy and the scatte
release of energy is the
ation. Thus, if there ha
beginning of our phys
to observe its effects in

In the early 1960s, Pen
ing for Bell Laboratorie
radiation in deep spa
the blast effect that mu
happened. Along with
data was being gathere
verse did have a beginn
with a tremendous explo
in the beginning, and ev
have come from a first c
God; "And God said, Let

Philosophically, if every
then that first cause is a
but *it*. Theology calls it (
Once he had confirmed
whether the universe
seemed to be coming up
verse did have a beginn
Christianity teaches that

beginning a
a first cause
of the unive
day. Furthe
universe bac
night. These
cosmic night

In order to e
came from,
This theory
verse. It stat
slows down,
rest. Howeve
gravitational
come back t
egg might t
births and d
have made
believe that
to collapse,

Looking ba
over again,
accurate th
sensation c
recall the c
"As it was
without en
resounded
body! In es
arrangeme
the unkno
knew that

AM I A MIND?

Robert had come to the conclusion that he was not just a body. He had a body, but he was something more. He was some part of the unknown. Robert began to research books on theology, psychology, philosophy and metaphysics. He noted some of the conclusions reached by others concerning this unknown essence, and he became conscious of the terms *universal mind* and *infinite mind*.

Reflecting on these terms caused Robert to consider whether or not he was a mind. He began to recall his experience with the subject of mind. It had started during his high school days when he and his classmates would travel to Middletown, New York to watch their school team compete. One evening, while attending a dance after the game, Robert met and became acquainted with a girl whose father was a doctor at the state hospital for the mentally ill.

After their initial meeting, Robert began dating the girl quite regularly and, as a result, became well acquainted with her parents. During his many visits to their home, Robert had several conversations with the girl's father regarding patients who had 'lost their minds'. He wondered how a person could lose their mind. He reasoned that if one could lose something that belonged to him, then he was not that which had been lost. Therefore, it seemed logical to Robert that if one can lose his mind, then he cannot be the mind.

As he read further on this subject, Robert became thoroughly confused by authors who wrote that the mind is God. To Robert this implied that one who had lost his mind had lost God. Years later, he was still trying to figure out just what the mind was. He became determined to find his own definition since he had not been able to find a satisfactory one anywhere else.

Robert had been told that in order to have a mind, one must have a brain. Since only humans and animals had a brain, they were the only life forms that could possess a mind. Therefore, wanting to understand the mind, Robert started to research the brain as to its function, creation and evolution. He discovered that the brain controlled all the functions of the body. Further, humans and animals became conscious of their environment through the five physical senses, and this awareness was registered on the brain cells. As forms developed, they gained a greater awareness of their environment due to a larger and more complex brain.

During the nineteenth century, chemists had classified all matter into two major categories. The first category consisted of matter that, when heated, broke down completely and changed irreversibly. The second category consisted of matter that, when heated, remained basically unchanged. The first category was comprised of all matter in living, animate forms, and the second category was comprised of inanimate matter such as water, minerals and gas. At one time, most scientists believed that no matter could be both animate and inanimate, but rather, it had to be one or the other.

A Swedish chemist named Berzelious named animate matter *organic* and *inanimate* matter inorganic. Today, the study of animate matter is known as *organic chemistry* and the study of inanimate matter is known as *inorganic chemistry*. Berzelious made the statement that organic compounds could only come from living substances. However, it was not long after that Friedrich Wholer, a student of

Berzelious, made a discovery that challenged his teacher's theory. Wholer discovered that some inorganic substances could be changed into organic substances. By applying heat to ammonium cyanate, an inorganic substance, he was able to produce an organic substance called urea, a major component of urine. This disproved Berzelious' earlier statement and forever changed how scientists differentiated living from non-living matter.

After this classification was broken down, scientists were no longer restricted to thinking that they could not create organic materials from inorganic matter. From that time on, chemical research flourished in the area of synthesizing naturally occurring organic substances. As a result of this research, scientists created many synthetic products, such as rubber, nylon, plastics and drugs that mimic naturally occurring counterparts.

Sir Isaac Newton revealed and defined an attribute of all matter called *gravity*. This attribute was defined in his law, which stated that every unit of matter attracts every other unit to some degree. In spite of the investigation of science into the properties of matter, scientists failed to fully understand gravity. More appropriate words should have been used in Newton's definition. This attribute should have been defined as *awareness*. It is the awareness within matter that creates the force of attraction between all units of it.

All matter, from the simplest units within atoms to humans, the most highly developed forms, manifests different degrees of awareness. Awareness in matter is the inherent ability of that body to receive and respond to stimuli from the environment. The response of the form to outside stimuli through the awareness is its *life*.

Electrically charged subatomic particles either attract or repel one another. This response of attraction and repulsion is the life expressing through these particles. Because this is the only awareness within the subatomic particles, this behavior is the only expression of life they manifest. The forces of attraction and repulsion have built the entire universe. These forces are nothing more than a lower degree of what man calls love and hate.

In the early stages of evolution, after all the inanimate forms had been created, the first single-celled organisms of animate life developed. Within each of these organisms was a central nucleus surrounded by other materials. These cells might be considered as more advanced replicas of atoms. A cell that did not possess a nucleus, such as a red blood cell, was unable to grow or divide, and therefore, was unable to generate new cells. From this it was obvious that the awareness of reproduction was locked within the nucleus of the cell. Each cell possessed its own awareness and expressed its own life. In order to further evolve, cells integrated with each other to form more advanced multi-cellular organisms. Because each cell had its own awareness, the life expression of the new multi-cellular organism was influenced by each individual cell's response.

The banding together of the original Thirteen Colonies of America is a good illustration of cell integration on a much higher level. After the Thirteen Colonies had gained their independence from England, they each wanted to go their own way. This would have left each of them isolated and weak, and eventually they would have lost the freedom that each had gained. After assembling to discuss their mutual needs, each colony was willing to give up some of its rights in favor of a stronger, unified government.

While this seemed to be a new idea, it was exactly what happened during the Earth's history when single cells combined to form more highly developed organisms. As greater multi-cellular organisms evolved, it became necessary for them to develop a common communication system. These communication links were formed when the fibers sent out from different cells fused together. As more highly developed organisms evolved, it became necessary to form a communication network from a central receiving station to each cell.

There is scientific evidence which suggests that touch was the first sense to be conveyed through this communication network. Each single cell had an awareness of forms outside itself because of this sense. In their struggle for food and survival, these organisms were gaining awareness of their changing environment. Some cells in the organisms became more sensitive to light, other cells more sensitive to smells, others to tastes, and others to sounds. Ultimately, groups of these specialized cells became what are now recognized as the sense organs.

These rudimentary sense organs became new avenues to gain greater awareness. The flatworm was one of the earliest creatures to possess these sense organs, which were located in its head. The first awareness of the flatworm's environment was gained as it moved about. Instead of affecting the cells of its entire body, this awareness was conveyed from its head, through nerve channels, only to those parts of its body where the response was needed. This centralization of the communication network was the beginning of the brain and the central nervous system.

As higher forms of life evolved, the sense organs became more sensitive and the brain increased its capacity to be more aware and more responsive, thus giving the forms greater life. The forms gained more information from the stimuli of the environment through the five senses. This increased awareness enabled the brain to transmit greater amounts of information to the body more quickly. This resulted in greater protection for the animal. It also gave the animal a greater life expression, and thus, greater freedom.

As the central nervous system became more highly developed, a sheath formed around it for protection. In time, the sheath became the spine or backbone, and this backbone became the main girder for the building of the skeletal system of all higher animals.

The rudimentary brain developed into a forebrain, a midbrain and a hindbrain. The forebrain recorded the senses of smell and taste and was divided into sections, the cerebrum being the largest. At the top of the cerebrum was the cerebral cortex. The cerebrum eventually became more dominant, while the midbrain and hindbrain became less significant. As the brain increased in size, its smooth surface began to develop folds or twisted cords called *convolutions*. It was these convolutions that allowed a greater capacity for awareness in the brain. The brain not only responded to its environment but also retained the awareness of all the experiences of the organism. This previous awareness, stored in the brain, extended all the way back to the awareness of attraction and repulsion in the subatomic particles of the atom.

Also stored in the brain was awareness of the organization of molecules, the reproduction and growth of both plants and animals, and the ability to build the nest of the bird, the dam of the beaver, and the hive of the bee. In order to survive, the animal had to fight or flee from its enemies and, as a result, fear and anger became instinctive emotions stored as awareness on the brain. Selfishness, greed and even vanity became expressions of life in the animal. All this awareness of the environment was impressed on the animal's brain without it being conscious. The response of the animal to environmental stimuli came from the awareness on the brain. It was beyond the animal's ability to change its instinctive responses. The animal was unable to interfere with its awareness because of the conditioned reflexes that instinctively guided it.

It was the inherited knowledge gained during the evolution of each species that caused a bird to build a nest, the spider to weave a web, and a young chick to break its shell. New characteristics that resulted in the advancement and survival of the form were passed on genetically and were retained in the awareness of future forms of the species. For example, when single cells united to form multi-cellular organisms, the very knowledge of uniting became a permanent part of the awareness within all subsequent forms of its kind. At first, the brain acted as a central switchboard in order to communicate feeling between different cells. Gradually, it developed further in order to be able to retain the awareness it received from the senses. One specific area of the brain developed in order to register impressions from each of the senses: sight, hearing, taste, touch and smell.

Each sense impression of sight, hearing, taste, touch and smell is called a *percept*. An object may first be perceived through the sense of sight. If so, a percept of this object is registered on cells in the area of the brain where only sight impressions are received. Similar objects are also registered in this same area as individual percepts. For example, when a tree is first seen, an individual sight impression of it becomes a percept on awareness. Every additional sight of other trees also becomes an individual percept in the same area of the brain. One might expect that, sooner or later, single percepts would impress all the cells in a specific area of the brain. However, instead of impressing more and more cells, the pre-existing cells, with similar percepts implanted on them, link together. Just as cells unite to form multi-cellular organisms, percepts join together to form *recepts*. A recept is a collection of percepts that defines an object from the sense impressions and allows an organism to respond in a specific way to a specific stimulus. Continuing with the above example, after the percepts have linked together and a new tree is seen, the awareness recognizes the impression as a generic tree, the recept, rather than a specific, individual tree.

Gradually, as more and more percepts and recepts develop, all the sense areas of the brain are linked with one another. This process was recently understood through many experiments concerning animal behavior. A good example is Pavlov's conditioned response experiments. When a dog has been temporarily deprived of food and is then shown food, it begins to salivate. In this particular experiment, prior to offering the dog some food, a bell is rung. After repetition, the dog's awareness associates being fed with the ringing of a bell. Eventually, the dog begins to salivate as soon as the bell is rung, just as though the actual food has been set in front of him. Because man has a conceptual brain, he is able to condition the dog. This proves that the dog has only a perceptual-receptual brain.

When two or more associated sense impressions are linked together in the brain as a word-picture association, the resultant creation is called a *concept*. Only the human brain has the ability to form concepts, and thus, only man can classify concepts, positively or negatively, and create his own inner mental world.

If one has knowledge of percepts, recepts and concepts, they can readily observe sequential steps in the development of a child. First, sense impressions become percepts, next these percepts link together to form recepts and finally concepts. As the child reaches the age when sense impressions are associated and forms concepts of self, the child receives 'the breath of life' and becomes a self-conscious individual.

Not only does science prove this, but the *Genesis* account of creation also mentions this developmental process. The Bible states that, "...man became a living soul," and, "Let us make man in our image, after our likeness". One might ask what is meant by, "...in our image, after our likeness". Man has concluded, by observing his own form and shape, that God was made in the image of man. In itself, it demands that God be physical. Throughout the Old Testament, God is even described as having all the weaknesses of man, such as being jealous, angry and even wrathful. From the *Genesis* story, one discovers that the outstanding ability of God is that of being a creator. We now know that animals, through instinct, can build physical things. But we also know that they are unable to form mental images, thoughts or concepts, so as to have them manifest on the physical plane. It seems that *only* man can gather ideas, put them together and impress them as an image upon his brain cells. If he dwells upon the image long enough, the force of the image will cause him or her to carry it out, just as an ingrained habit is carried out automatically in his or her life.

The laws by which an impressed image manifests are demonstrated and proven by hypnosis. In hypnosis, the operator must first get the subject's attention. After getting the subject to listen, he can impress a suggestion upon the subject's brain with such force that after the subject is brought back to a normal state, the suggestion, now known as a post-hypnotic suggestion, will incline the subject to carry it out.

In *Genesis*, it states that Adam named the animals. It also states that Adam and Eve were the only creatures of God that were forbidden to eat of the tree of the knowledge of good and evil. Man's brain is designed so that he forms concepts by associating a word with a picture or a recept. Further, these concepts are classified according to his personal experiences with them. Every human being can and does classify his experiences as they affect him. In this way, the beautiful world of God is destroyed as each individual unconsciously classifies and lives in his own created world.

In recent years, man has developed the computer. The computer stores in its memory bank the information fed or programmed into it as electrical charges. When a question, translated into electrical impulses, is fed into this computer that is in resonance with information already stored in its memory bank, information will be sent out from the computer in the form of an answer.

Scientists have discovered, when working with animal and human brains, that brain cells also send out electrical charges, which have been recorded as brain waves. The techniques now employed by biofeedback are based upon the fundamental principle that the brain is an electrical instrument. Furthermore, it is now known that our sense organs, such as our eyes, transmute environmental energy into electrical energy. This transformed energy amplifies our brain cells, bringing the information from the subconscious to consciousness.

To explain this in another way, consider television. After transmuting sights and sounds into electrical energy, a station sends the energy over a designated wave. Any television set that is capable of being in resonance with this wave receives the electrical signals that are carried by the wave and transmutes the signals back into sights and sounds. There are only two ways that sound coming from the television can be heard clearly. One way is to increase the volume using the volume control. The other way is to shut out all outside noises so that the less amplified sounds can be heard. Another thing we can do with a television set is to change channels so that we can tune into the frequency of other stations.

Similarly, our brain is an instrument much like a television set. Through our sense organs, the brain receives impressions of the environment. The sense organs transmute the energy that comes from the environment into electrical signals, which are then carried to the brain cells, amplifying them so that we become conscious as listeners and observers.

In order to prove to himself that his findings on the activity of the brain were true, Robert performed a very simple experiment. Using only his imagination, he visualized, as clearly as possible, going to the refrigerator. He picked up a lemon and felt its smooth surface. Next he cut the lemon and observed, in his imagination, some of the juice coming to the surface. He then squeezed the lemon, filling a glass with its juice. He held the glass up to the light and saw the clearness of the juice and the foam that had formed on top. Finally, he slowly raised the glass to his lips and drank it down. To his amazement, his mouth filled with saliva just as though the imaginary drink of lemon juice was real!

Now he knew! As a result of his experiments and research, Robert knew that he was *not* the mind. He was that *something* that had the ability to use imagination and to program his own brain. Robert realized that, in fact, man has no mind. What he had referred to as *mind* was simply the activity of brain cells. Man was not this activity! He was something much, much more. He was that which could observe and direct that activity.

AM I A SOUL?

Robert felt slightly intoxicated, as though he had been drinking wine. He felt he was 'spinning' in space. He was so elated at what he had found that his feelings of wonder were beyond description! However, immediately following his elation, Robert had a sobering thought. He realized that if he were to discuss these things with anyone, they would probably say that he had lost his mind. By now, he had concluded that he did not have a mind, but he did have a brain and he understood its activity. Robert therefore reasoned that he could not lose that which he did not have.

Once again Robert recalled making the sign of the cross while repeating, "In the name of the Father, and of the Son, and of the Holy Spirit, Amen." He also remembered the statements in *The Gospel According to St. John.*

> *In the beginning was the Word, and the Word was with God, and the Word was God. The same was in the beginning with God. All things were made by him; and without him was not any thing made that was made. In him was life; and the life was the light of men.*

Many theologians accept the Trinity of God. Christianity states that there is only one God, but that God consists of three parts: the Father, the Son and the Holy Spirit. This was an enigma for Robert. He wondered how he could account for one God being three persons in the light of what he had already discovered. Back to the Bible and science he went, and after much research and contemplation, he found that the Bible and science again agreed.

Just as theology says that there is only one God, science has proven that there is only one essential essence pervading the entire universe. Many theologies describe God as having three forms. Robert wondered if there was a similar trinity in science, describing energy. Science has proven that energy takes at least two forms: energy and matter. Even the smallest subatomic particles are packets of energy called *quanta*, and these units are constantly in motion. Science reveals that all physical forms are composed of mass and energy. Further, the packets of energy or particles, of which the body is composed, respond to outside particles or forces that cause the reactions of attraction and repulsion. Science has studied the reaction of these particles to forces and has proposed theories concerning them. They suggest that that which causes this reaction is a third nature or aspect of energy. After reading material on this subject, Robert immediately recognized that science was speculating on the existence and function of awareness in matter. Robert knew that the inherent ability in matter to respond to the outside environment is the matter's awareness. To Robert, these three aspects of energy correlated perfectly with the theological concept of the Holy Trinity.

After correlating *The Gospel of St. John* and the findings of science, Robert then speculated that in the beginning, this total essence was in one central body or mass, alone in the void. If this was true, then all the mass, all the energy and all the awareness that ever existed and that will ever exist was there in the beginning, within itself. Science has proven that energy is both a cause and an effect of itself. Potential energy (stored up energy) can be changed into kinetic energy (moving energy), and this moving energy can again be added to mass and become stored up again. When potential energy is released and becomes kinetic energy, it is changed into bundles or quanta in the form of photons of radiant energy. Some of these quanta subsequently change back into matter in the form of protons, neutrons, electrons, positrons, neutrinos, etc.

These primary building blocks attract or repel each other due to the awareness in each, and these reactions result in the formation of atoms. From the atoms come the elements. In turn, due to the arrangement and organization of the atoms, all molecules and compounds, indeed all matter, is created. When molecules of matter gain greater awareness, they develop the ability to replicate, which eventually leads to reproduction and growth. Each successively higher creation gains greater and greater awareness, until finally a creation comes upon the scene, which becomes conscious of this awareness within itself.

Genesis stated, "And the Lord God formed man of the dust of the ground, and breathed into his nostrils the breath of life; and man became a living soul." Robert wondered what the soul really was. *Genesis* also stated that, "...man became a living soul." It did not say that man *was* a soul. Robert started to feel quite amused because he remembered a situation he had gotten himself into in the seventh grade. He recalled it as though it occurred yesterday.

His class had just finished their daily Catechism lesson conducted by the priest. Before the Father could leave the class, Robert stepped in front of him. "Father," he asked, "Am I a soul?"

"Why yes, my son, you are a soul," the priest said.

"Father," said Robert, "Sister says I must live the church laws.

Will it save my soul?"

"Not only for that reason, son, but also to assure that your soul will go to heaven when you die."

"Father, from what you say then, I must have a soul. Is that right?"

"That's correct, my lad."

"Father, I'm confused. First you told me that I was a soul, now you tell me that I have one. I don't understand, Father! How can I have a soul and still be a soul? Father, which one is it?" With this last question the Father stood there bristling. He became so exasperated that he told Robert to never, never question him again. Recalling this event, Robert knew that if he went to the theologians with what he then knew, they would likely be even more hostile towards him. He knew, however, that he would not discover many of the answers concerning the soul from science.

The basic source of information in theology is derived from various religious texts. For instance, if Robert were a Buddhist he would study the *Tripitaka*, the Buddhists' sacred text. If he were a Hindu, he would study the *Vedas,* and if he were a Muslim, the *Koran* would be his reference book. Since he was none of these, but had been reared in the Christian faith, his source of information continued to be the Bible.

Robert had already found that the Bible and science agreed regarding the creation of the universe. Going back to *The Book of Genesis*, however, he found two opposing accounts regarding the order in which things were created.

Chapter one of *The Book of Genesis* stated that God created the heavens, the earth, the plants, the animals, and finally, man. However, in chapter two, it stated that God created the heavens, the earth, man, the plants and finally the animals. Robert wondered how this could be! How could the Bible have errors if it were the inspired word of God? He read and reread these two accounts over and over, only to find that no matter how he approached it, the two accounts definitely contradicted each other.

Exploring these two chapters, he again found that God said, "Let us make man in our image, after our likeness: and let them have dominion over...all of the earth". In chapter two he read, "And the Lord God formed man of the dust of the ground, and breathed into his nostrils the breath of life; and man became a living soul." "Ahhhh," thought Robert, "here is the key I've been looking for, '...man became a living soul.'" If man became a living soul, he must have been something else before. What was he before? If man came before the animal, as was stated in the second chapter of Genesis, he must have been an evolving, conscious being. He must have had the awareness that eventually was to become awakened. Thus, the statement in Genesis that man had dominion over the fish, birds and the animals did not mean that man had dominion over their physical forms. Rather, man had a higher or dominant consciousness than that possessed by the animal.

This is not to imply that man has not inherited the beastly traits lodged within his subconscious depths, for he has. However, Jesus taught that man should overcome 'the beast within'. If all life is the expression through form of the awareness that has been impressed within the brain and body, then man, having the awareness of 'the beast within', must become conscious of his own acts, feelings and environment in order to overcome his animal nature. Man has within him fear, worry, anger, selfishness, greed, etc., all of which are attributes of 'the beast within'. It is this nature that man must master.

The Book of Genesis further states that, "But of the tree of knowledge of good and evil, thou shalt not eat of it: for in the day thou eatest thereof thou shalt surely die." To understand this, one must realize that experiences in his environment become impressed on his brain, and eventually, he becomes unconscious of them. In other words, the individual forgets an event, person, thing or experience, and the classifications of it. However, once an outside influence of similar nature activates the same awareness, the individual once again becomes conscious of the experience and its associated classifications.

Prior to Adam's (man's) appearance upon the scene, no other form was conscious of its own awareness or of its life. When an animal received outside stimuli through the senses, the awareness within was activated, causing the animal to react automatically. In other words, the animal itself did not know why or how it acted or reacted as it did. When Adam appeared upon the scene, he became conscious of the awareness and life expressing through him. Adam was tempted by Eve, his inner awareness, and he ate of the tree of knowledge of good and evil. Thereafter, everything that appeared to him in his consciousness was classified as either good or bad, as it affected him. In so doing, the inner guidance or instinct within man was stilled. It was turned off by the stronger influence of his limiting awareness. This resulted in the death of the inner guidance that had previously influenced him and which had no classifications.

Then, instead of seeing everything as good, as God saw it, man started classifying everything that affected him as either being good or evil. Man was no longer living in the Garden of Eden. He became enslaved to the pair of opposites.

Every thing, every thought and every act has dual aspects. Depending upon an individual's experience, it can be classified in one instance as being good and in another as being bad. In one's awareness, he or she can have two diametrically opposing associations linked to the same thing, thought or act. When the awareness is activated later, it brings to the individual's consciousness these opposing associations, causing him or her to select one over the other, instead of relying on an inner guidance that is heeded by all animal forms.

'The breath of life' that was breathed into man's form made him conscious of his body and mind, and made him self-conscious or a 'living soul'. The process of a young child becoming conscious of his own feelings, senses, and acts is represented by 'the breath of life' being breathed into his nostrils. Thereafter, the child refers to himself as 'I', a separate and distinct, self-conscious entity or soul.

The soul must have been created to become conscious of the life expressing through its form and to be able to master that life. However, instead of mastering the life within, man has classified it as being either good or bad. Therefore, while man should have become an awakened soul and the master of his lower self, he has remained asleep, and thus, enslaved to his limiting associations.

Jesus tried to give man a greater life by telling him that his sins were forgiven. If man would follow His teachings, they would lead him to a more abundant life. Jesus did not allow His lower nature, which was Satan, to influence Him. Instead, He listened to the voice within, which He called His Father, to guide and direct Him. He taught man how to rise above limitations and thereby walk in the path of righteousness as He did.

After all his findings, Robert concluded that he was a 'living soul'. He was not a body or a mind but 'a living soul', made 'in the image and likeness of God'. Further, all souls were his brothers. Robert's thoughts went back to the most tragic and unforgettable incident of his youth. This one incident supported, more than any other, that he was an essential unit of the Divine Trinity: body, spirit and soul.

Robert's mother had an unusual gift. She would often experience what were known as premonitions. She was able to foretell, with great accuracy, the events that were to take place in the lives of others, and she was quite noted for her ability. For example, she was asked to don a gypsy costume and read fortunes at a bazaar in the Audubon Center to help raise funds for the construction of the New York Medical Center at 168th Street in New York City.

One morning, during the summer of 1939, Robert got up earlier than usual. When he came downstairs, he found his mother sitting at the breakfast table looking quite distressed. Robert asked her what was wrong, and she began relating a dream she had had the night before. She said, "Robbie, I will not be here to celebrate my next birthday. Last night, I saw myself laid out in a mahogany casket. The lining was a peach colored, satin material. Over the closed portion of the casket was a blanket of yellow roses with 'Mother' written on it. And, Robbie, there was an unusual object, against the lining, inside the raised lid. I couldn't make out what it was, but it glowed in the dark." After this, she went on to describe other floral pieces that had been placed around her casket. Two weeks later, on a Saturday afternoon, it started to rain. Because the housekeeper was gone for the afternoon, Mrs. Casper started to take a load of wash off the clothesline. As she was pulling the line, it broke, and the force of it knocked her to the ground. She immediately started to suffer severe pain, and was quickly rushed to the hospital. Upon examining her, the doctors discovered that she had sustained a rupture. During the operation it was discovered that she also had gallstones. The doctors proceeded to remove her gall bladder.

For a few days after the surgery, Mrs. Casper was recovering rapidly. Then, all at once, her temperature began to soar and she died within twenty-four hours. Her death occurred just two weeks before her fortieth birthday. The doctors had made a serious mistake by performing two operations at the same time. This was before penicillin and other similar antibiotics, and so, the doctors were unable to prevent the spread of infection from one area to the other. It was reported that peritonitis was the cause of her death.

Mrs. Casper's body was brought home for the funeral service. While his father and sister were attending to all the arrangements, Robert was busy sending wires and running back and forth, transporting relatives and close friends. The evening that his mother was laid out, he had to drive to the station again to pick up a few latecomers. Soon after he returned home, he walked to the parlor door and paused there, dreading to go in. He and his mother had been so very close. As he caught sight of the front of the casket, he immediately went into shock. There, in the lid of the casket was the glowing object his mother had described in her dream.

The next morning, Robert had to be led back into the parlor. There, in front of him, was the mahogany casket, the blanket of yellow roses, the peach colored, satin lining and the object in the lid. The object he had seen glowing the night before was a crucifix. He later learned that reflectors, such as this one, were just starting to be used by funeral directors. Robert later verified that neither his father nor his sister had been told of his mother's dream. She had told Robert "not to tell a soul," swearing him to secrecy.

This whole experience resulted in Robert wanting to study science in every aspect in order to comprehend his mother's gift. Since he was already enrolled in college, he had every opportunity to do so. What was it that his mother had possessed that enabled her to foretell the future? It had to be something beyond the senses, beyond her physical body, beyond her mind. Could it be something that science could explain?

It wasn't until years later that Robert was able to understand his mother's gift. She had a strong inner guidance. To some degree, she had become an awakened soul, which allowed her to become conscious of her inner guidance. Robert eventually came to an understanding of the nature of this rare gift. He then came to the conclusion that he was not a body, nor a mind, but was 'a living soul', made 'in the image and likeness of God'. In addition, Robert knew that all mankind is part of the infinite Creative Essence, being a trinity of body, soul and spirit.

PART II

Why Am I Here?

WHY AM I HERE?

Sooner or later in an individual's life, one knowingly or unknowingly, asks himself two questions: why am I here and what is the purpose of my life? Robert was no exception. Although Robert had never had a mystical experience of any kind, at least not the kind talked of or written about, he had come to the conclusion that all humans are special creations of the one creative essence.

Robert had decided that his study of metaphysics and its extensive branches could wait. He could investigate them later. He knew that he existed but he realized that metaphysics could not explain the purpose for his existence. With this in mind, he began again to review some of the main events that had transpired in his life.

Robert recalled the eight long years in elementary school when he learned the basics for further education. During this time, his teachers judged him as to his learning ability, and if he did not take home a good report card, his parents punished him. The only time Robert really felt any degree of freedom was during his summer vacations. The reason for Robert's lack of enthusiasm for school was, in his mind, due to the limited approach of his teachers.

Among other subjects at school, he was taught reading and writing English. These particular subjects were important as they gave him the knowledge and means by which he could communicate with and understand others. However, much of the data he was taught caused him confusion in later years. One example was history. Many students believed, without a doubt, that the accounts of our great presidents, our great generals and statesmen were factual! As the students grew older, they found that there were 'gaping holes' in some of these stories. Furthermore, those children who attended Sunday school were taught lessons that caused them to become prejudiced and biased.

Most students then spent the next four years in high school. By then, they learned that they had to agree with their teachers' views and the textbooks in order to get good grades. In other words, they were not allowed to think freely! If they did think for themselves, they were penalized. Someone must have been doing some thinking, however, because these same textbooks eventually became either obsolete or revised.

Robert recalled having to write an essay on Shakespeare's play, *As You Like It*, in his high school English class. His assignment was to explain what the play was all about and to summarize what Shakespeare had in mind. Robert wrote, "I do not know what Shakespeare had in mind when he wrote *As You Like It*. He has been dead for a long time now, and as a result, I have not had the opportunity to interview him." It came as no surprise to Robert that he received a failing grade on his assignment. This was not to happen a second time.

The next essay assignment was on the story, *Silas Marner*. Each night for homework, the class was required to read a certain portion of the story in order to be prepared for the following day's group discussion. In these open discussions, Robert made doubly sure that he listened intently to his teacher's dissertations, her remarks and her opinions. After the story was completely read and discussed, it was time to write his essay. Robert wrote and wrote, but it wasn't *his* essay he was writing. It was his teacher's! At every turn of the story, it was her opinions that flowed from his pen. It came as no surprise to him that this time he received a perfect grade on his paper. Robert learned from this incident alone that to think independently was to bring destruction upon oneself. To be an obedient follower without questioning was to save oneself.

Each individual has their own personal memories of school, and from these memories, one gradually develops many fixed ideas regarding life in general. As a result of personal experiences, each person's awareness becomes individualized and eventually becomes his or her personal ego. And so, it might be said that four years of high school means four years of learning to become more separated from the one life. Furthermore, those who are less fortunate than others, go to work immediately after high school, ending their formal education. This separation causes some to develop inferiority complexes. Others go on to college and some develop superiority complexes. These feelings of inferiority and superiority cause us to become more and more separated. In the Scriptures, and even in the Declaration of Independence, it states that all men are created equal. These beautiful words are true but are not understood by one who sees himself as a separate individual.

Normally, after formal education, one is expected to take his or her place in the work force as tradition dictates. However, this was not true during the war years. After completing his college education, Robert was inducted into the armed forces to fight in World War II. There, he was trained to kill the enemy in order to help save his country, and thus, restore peace to the world. Many of his most cherished dreams and plans 'went up in smoke'. During this period of his life, Robert continued to ask himself several questions: why am I here, what is the purpose of my life, what is my future, and what the hell is life all about?

During the war years, thousands of young, educated men were mowed down like animals before they even had a chance to find out what life was all about and be free. Why? Robert thought it was the cruelest irony that they had grown up only to come to this horrible end.

MY TREE OF KNOWLEDGE

As a result of the terrible carnage Robert witnessed during the war, he began to question his faith in God. Knowing that many men were being killed everyday and thinking that his name could be added to that 'great honor roll in the sky', Robert came to the conclusion that all he had been taught about God and His mercy was pure fantasy. Robert renounced it all! If God were all good and all merciful, as Robert had been taught to believe, how could He allow this terrible destruction to take place? How could He allow the destruction of His highest creation?

Because of his lack of conviction that God existed, Robert realized that he had a major conflict to resolve within himself. One of the established army programs was for soldiers to attend the religious services of their choice. The army provided separate services for each religious denomination. Being a Second Lieutenant, Robert knew that in order to be an effective officer, he had to set a good example for his men to follow. How could he encourage his men to attend chapel if he did not? If he did encourage his men to attend chapel, his own refusal to attend the services would make him a hypocrite in the eyes of his men. Yet if he did attend the services, having renounced God, he would be a hypocrite in his own eyes. What was he to do? Was he right? Was his renunciation valid? Had his decision, made in deep bitterness, been too hasty?

In order to re-think his decision and to resolve his dilemma, he knew that he had to investigate further. Robert knew some individuals who were sincere in their religious convictions and who seemed to have gained something that he lacked. Further, having listened to the chaplains, with their sincerity and enthusiasm, Robert began to reason that they must have achieved their convictions through study of the Bible. He recalled that somewhere in the Bible is the statement that we are admonished to study the Scriptures. The Bible states, "Know the truth and the truth will make you free". Therefore, the urgency of his situation, coupled with his investigative nature, caused Robert to delve into his government issued Bible.

During his deep search, it dawned upon Robert that the biblical stories must have a literal or exoteric meaning. Because of these literal or exoteric meanings, the Bible seemed confusing and appeared to be contradictory. Upon further investigation, Robert discovered that these seemingly literal stories were not literal at all; the stories were allegorical and behind each there was a hidden, esoteric meaning. Robert then understood why Jesus had advised his followers to study the Scriptures.

No one before Jesus had ever revealed that there was more than one meaning to the biblical stories. Jesus told his followers that He taught them in parables, and that behind each parable was a truth that could be understood if they only had the ears to hear and the eyes to see. After much study and long, careful deliberation, Robert started to regain the conviction he had had in his childhood. Robert then felt that the teachings of Jesus were true, and thus, his faith in his 'hero' was restored.

While studying the Bible, Robert began to perceive the esoteric truths common to all Christian denominations. He then felt free to attend various denominational services with his men, not just the Catholic services. With his newfound freedom and an open mind, Robert hoped that he would find the keys that would help to unlock the inner meanings of the Bible. He then had the opportunity to break any enslavement he might have had to the religion into which he was born. Furthermore, Robert's attendance set a good example for his men, not only to attend the Sunday service of their choice but also to be tolerant of other denominational faiths.

For many years, his search for hidden meanings in the Bible continued to play a dominant role in Robert's life. One day, after the war was over, he was sitting outdoors at his home when he heard a voice! It was such a startling experience he wondered if he were losing his mind. Robert knew he was not crazy; he *had* heard a voice! The voice said to him, "Get the Bible and read the first few chapters of *Genesis* concerning creation." Immediately, he got out of his lawn chair, found his Bible and read the account of how God had created the entire universe in six days.

When he had finished, the voice returned and asked, "What is a day in eternity?" This question reminded him of a passage that he had once read somewhere in the Bible, that a day in eternity was like a thousand years on earth. The early writers of the Scriptures must have thought that a thousand years was a vast, incomprehensible period of time. With this new understanding, Robert was able to change his own concept that a day in the Bible meant a limited, fixed period of time. He concluded that a day in eternity must have meant a phase or stage of creation.

As he studied further, it became clear to Robert that the *Genesis* story was a description of the evolution of life. It conformed to scientific evidence and accepted theories.

This revelation gave Robert a new understanding. He realized that the word *man* or *Adam* referred to all individual, evolving souls. Adam and Eve were like children who at first did not know the difference between good and bad, and who lived in the beautiful Garden of Eden. We were all guided and inclined by God until a separating wall came between God and us. This separation occurred as our personal egos developed.

It was then apparent to Robert that as one grew out of childhood, the awareness of the environment caused him to classify all things, thoughts, and actions as they affected him. All these things were classified as either good or evil, depending on one's personal experiences. Adam and Eve's eating from the tree of knowledge of good and evil symbolized the process of classification. Adam, like all individuals, began to see his world dualistically rather than seeing all expressions of life as one. As a result, many classified concepts were impressed upon his brain. Those things in his life that were beneficial or pleasurable were classified as good, and all things that were detrimental or painful were classified as bad.

Early man was like a child in that he did not classify any thing, thought or action, and was guided only by instinct. Eventually, instead of being inclined by only one instinctive voice from within, man was also inclined by his classifications of sensory impressions from his environment. As a result, he could not distinguish between the inner voice of instinct and his own concepts of good and evil. Consequently, man no longer lived in the Garden of Eden, the place of perfect peace, and his own classifications battled against the natural, directive 'voice of God'. Man no longer listened to this instinctive guidance and had to evaluate it against his own acquired concepts. In the Bible, this was referred to as having to work by 'the sweat of thy face'. Man was kicked out of the Garden of Eden due to his classification of life as good or evil, causing him to separate himself from the oneness of life. Contrary to what religion taught, the original sin that was inherited by all individuals was the classification of life. Most Christian religions taught that this original sin would only be forgiven with the coming of a savior.

Late that evening, Robert heard the voice again. This time it directed him to read the last book of the Bible, *The Book of Revelation*. None of it seemed to make sense to Robert, except the part relating the end of the world to the Second Coming of Christ. Robert remembered having read somewhere in the Bible that when Christ came, He would come, "...in all His glory". The voice then asked, "What is His glory?" At first, Robert had no answer.

Robert pondered on this question until he finally came to a conclusion. He realized that the Second Coming did not mean that Jesus would return to the Earth in physical form. Rather, he realized that the great glory of Christ, the teachings that Jesus gave us, will return to the consciousness of man and be made understandable. His teachings will show mankind how to return to the garden and partake of the 'tree of life', thus raising the consciousness of those who are spiritually dead into life everlasting. Jesus was raised in consciousness to become the Christ, the anointed teacher, whose teachings could remove the original sin of man. These teachings could show man the way back to the Garden of Eden, the Kingdom of Heaven within us all.

This experience changed Robert's entire outlook on life. From that time forward, he resolved to study the teachings of Jesus intensely in order to understand fully the knowledge he had gained during his wonderful, enlightening experience. Robert knew that the study would be long and difficult. Even Jesus' twelve Apostles did not understand Him, despite His efforts to give them the keys to the Kingdom of Heaven.

Robert knew that besides unlocking doors, keys could also be clues to solving mysteries. He was determined to discover the keys that Jesus had tried to communicate to his Apostles. Robert began to search the Bible for any keys that could help solve the mystery of why he existed.

Jesus said that He spoke in parables, in exoteric stories. Robert had come to the conclusion that man's understanding of the parables depended upon the level of consciousness he possessed. If one interpreted any statements from a personal, self-conscious point-of-view, he would only be capable of gaining exoteric knowledge. An understanding of the esoteric meanings of the biblical stories could only be gained from a universal, one life point-of-view.

Contemplating these ideas, Robert began to visualize himself as Adam in the Garden of Eden. First, he ate of the tree of the knowledge of good and evil. Having committed this original sin of classification, Adam was no longer in God's good graces. To hide from God and to cover up his guilt, he donned a garment of fig leaves. Robert realized that this interpretation of the story was limited. He knew that there had to be a deeper meaning to this story, so he began to ponder on the actions of Adam in the garden. If Adam had not eaten of the tree of knowledge, but instead had just blindly obeyed the inclinations from within him, would he have become anything different? Would he have remained just like an animal, guided strictly by instincts from within? But Adam *did* eat the fruit and was no longer only guided by his instincts.

Robert recalled from the Scriptures that all men were made 'in the image and likeness of God'. Robert then reasoned that if God was the creator, and all men were created in His image and likeness, then all men were also creators. However, Robert recognized that not all of man's actions were conscious creations. He realized that his actions were also governed and influenced by the awareness from within him. It was this awareness from the environment that restricted his ability to reason correctly. Without exercising choice, man lived by instinct alone and could never make any original creations. He was like a living robot, blindly obeying the awareness within and remaining ignorant of the tree of knowledge in the garden.

Robert asked, "Am I to live by instinct alone? Am I to be a living robot and blindly obey the order, 'Thou shalt not eat of the tree of knowledge'?" No! If Robert was to be a creator and was to understand why he was here, he had to eat of the tree of knowledge and had to use reason over instinct.

Being a creator, but without full knowledge and understanding of the one life, man classified things, thoughts and acts. The Bible stated that God looked out upon His wonderful creation and classified it all as being good. Therefore, man's classification was contrary to the way God looked upon His creation. By classifying, man lost the perfect peace of being guided by instinct alone. Because of these classifications, man began to consider himself as having a personal, individual life. His only sin was this ignorance that caused him to become a single-celled, separate being.

Robert reasoned that if man had not classified life, he would still be in touch with that instinctive guidance within. The 'voice of God' or instinctive guidance consisted of all the inherited awareness from the beginning of life. Each individual was born with all the awareness of life before him. All awareness that had ever been gained was conserved. It was genetically passed on to each successive creation and was stored as inherited awareness.

Like other creations, man's brain also has impressed upon it the inherited awareness of all life before it. The brain also has the capacity to acquire new awareness from the environment. This awareness, in the form of sensory data, is impressed upon the brain cells. For this reason, the brain is like a fertile field that receives seeds from the environment, or a blank cassette tape that receives magnetic impressions. Everything that we have experienced since birth and every sensory impression that has come to us from the environment is received and stored in the brain.

Robert recognized that his parents and the rest of his family were the most influential authorities in his early life. They created and developed his concept of separateness during his early years. All of Robert's concepts of self-consciousness developed from this starting point, and as time passed, other individuals created self-conscious concepts in Robert's awareness, building upon this foundation. Because each person influencing Robert had different classifications of things, thoughts and acts, Robert's inner world was colored with stronger and stronger degrees of separateness. In like manner, God's world of complete oneness was destroyed within each of us, and in its place, we each developed our own separate, isolated world.

Robert related this separation to the biblical story of Cain and Abel. Abel was symbolic of the soul that was capable of receiving instinctive guidance from within, hearing the 'voice of God'. However, the awareness of being instinctively guided was slain by the opposing concept, represented by Cain. Therefore, Cain symbolized the acquired awareness of separateness that was instilled by others. It was this awareness that overpowered the inherited, instinctive guidance of man.

The name a child is given at birth is the first classification that separates him from oneness. His name makes him a single, separated cell of life in his own home. Some children are treated kindly by one parent and ignored or punished by the other. This causes them to feel closer to one parent than the other and likewise develops separation between siblings. Thus, separation upon separation takes its toll on the consciousness of the child by distancing him from his inherited, instinctive guidance.

We are first given the concept that we are separate, single individuals. Next we are taught that we are part of a larger unit called the family. We soon discover, however, that many things, including association with different religions, separate families from each other. Robert recalled how he found out that he did not belong to the same religion as his neighbors. One day, Helen, a little girl who lived down the street, asked him what he was. Robert, in turn, asked his mother what he was, and she told him that he was a Catholic. Robert didn't know what Catholic meant, but the next day he told the little girl that he was a Catholic and then asked her what she was. Perhaps after having asked her mother, Helen told him that she was a Protestant. Not knowing what that meant either, Robert went to his mother and told her that Helen was a Protestant. His mother, with her limited religious concepts and prejudices, told him that he could no longer play with Helen.

Later, Robert came to understand that religious concepts have caused wider rifts between individuals, groups, societies and nations than anything else has. Robert recalled some of the illogical, religious concepts that people held. One day, as two men stood arguing about the existence of God, Robert overheard the comment, "Thank God I'm an atheist." At another time, Robert was discussing religion with a Catholic friend of his. The friend mentioned how much he hated the Jews. Robert replied that his friend was going to have a rough time when he got to heaven and found a rabbi named Peter holding the key to heaven's door.

Most people consider the atrocities committed during Hitler's regime to be the epitome of evil. However, there have been more bloody wars and more tortures inflicted upon the human race because of man's supposed 'love of God' than for any other reason. The Crusades, the Spanish Inquisition, the war in Ireland between Protestants and Catholics, and the conflicts in the Middle East are all examples of the cruelty imposed upon the masses because of religious zeal.

While religion has separated nation from nation and family from family, the way parents raise and discipline their children has also separated each individual from oneness. It is a known fact that every child craves attention and recognition from other people. This force or desire within all forms derives from the original creative principle of cells joining together in order to have greater expression. If a child doesn't get attention by doing what is considered good, he will perform acts that are considered bad in order to get the attention he craves. Even the fear of punishment does not override this need.

Years later, through personal observation, Robert discovered that attention, or lack of attention, was one of the biggest causes of illness. He also discovered that parents had the opinion that 'being good' was natural for a child and that 'being bad' was unnatural. Robert reasoned that children should receive the greatest attention when they did something 'good'. Unfortunately, it seemed to him that children usually received attention from a parent only when they did something 'bad'. When compared with how pets were treated, this seemed ridiculous to Robert. He knew that no one expected a pet to carry out its master's exact commands. When the animal did carry out the commands, however, the owner was usually very happy and made a big fuss over it. It seemed to Robert that a little child was deserving of at least the same attention as one would give to a pet. However, he realized that parents looked upon children as if they should know better, instead of realizing that the child had to gradually develop into a responsible, reasoning individual.

Concepts of separation are given to individuals when they are just toddlers. Being *unawakened* souls, they are not conscious that they have a choice and do not need to make classifications. How unfortunate it has been that mankind has generally been ignorant of his ability to choose and select what is impressed as awareness within his form. Because this ignorance has manifested on all levels of human society, separation has plagued man's history. Adam and Eve were cast out of paradise because of classification. Their only way back into the garden was to overcome their classifications by using *reason*, their greatest gift.

MY GREATEST GIFT

Through classification, man has separated himself from the consciousness of knowing that there is only one life. In order to return to the Garden of Eden and to the consciousness of oneness, man needs to rid himself of all classifications. Man's ability to reason allows him to break down classifications and, in so doing, to become free.

Wanting to expand his understanding and to gain a greater consciousness of oneness, Robert realized that he would have to apply reason to all of his fixed and limiting acquired awareness. During his reasoning, Robert reviewed his interpretation of the stories in the Scriptures, all that was taught to him in school and in church, and what his friends and family had taught him. Robert started by reviewing his understanding of how children develop separation.

At approximately five years of age, a child starts to develop a personal ego or self-consciousness from influences in addition to the family environment. By this time, he has already learned how to associate words with objects. These word associations have developed into the basis of his language. The country and culture into which a child is born will determine the language that he or she will speak. In America, most children learn the English language. In France, most learn French, and in Russia, most learn Russian. It is this diversity of language amongst cultures that has promoted separation, confusion, mistrust, hatred and even war.

Robert began reviewing the biblical account of creation in *Genesis*. He realized that God did not use labels to identify His creations. To make Adam conscious of the different expressions of the one life, God brought all the animals before Adam to name. Instead of being able to see all these animals as expressions of the one life, Adam classified each animal as having its own individual, separate life. However, he *did* have the ability to not classify things, thoughts and actions.

At night, when we are asleep, our senses are dormant and we are not conscious of the outside environment. We only become conscious of our dreams, which are in the form of pictures. These pictures, coming to us, without words or sounds, are the 'voice' of God within. Upon awakening, these pictures are distorted by our association of them with the language that we use to describe our dreams. God brings to man, like He did to Adam, pictures for us to name. Because our dreams are in the form of pictures that come from within, and because God is within, this may be why God is portrayed as the *all-seeing eye*.

Language is not the only factor that promotes separation and self-consciousness in children. Some children, more than others, realize that they have inborn talents for art, music and poetry, whereas other children have difficulty identifying talents in these areas. These differences lead to the classification of children by their parents and the classification of students by their teachers.

Some parents try to give their children a head start in their education by teaching them certain subjects that they will learn when they start school. As a result, these children are perceived as being more intelligent than others are. This leads their teachers to believe that the children with this previous training are somehow superior to those who have not received prior instruction. The teachers' perception of the apparent differences in intelligence of the children causes the teachers to react differently to each child. Furthermore, these different reactions cause certain children to feel superior to their classmates and cause other children to feel inferior. This is yet another situation in which separation develops between individuals, magnifying self-consciousness.

Every time a student receives a report card from their teachers, these classifications are reinforced. The reinforcement of these concepts, or any fixed idea for that matter, has nothing to do whatsoever with the development of that priceless gift called *reason*. It is reason that enables us to distinguish truth from falsehood. It enables us to be free by ridding ourselves of all ingrained, limiting concepts that hold us captive.

Robert realized that he had been taught many concepts in school that he had later disproved through reason and investigation. In all areas of his study, including science, mathematics, history and religion, he was taught to learn and even memorize large amounts of information. Although this knowledge had no real, lasting value, it still constituted a large part of his world. For example, Robert remembered his historical study of General Custer's last stand. Robert was taught that Custer and his troops were forced into a valley before the Indians came swooping down upon them from the nearby hills. According to the story, the entire outfit was ambushed and massacred. Robert believed this story until he had the opportunity of visiting the actual battleground where Custer and his troops had fought. It was there that Robert learned what really happened! In truth, General Custer and his troops were on a hill, not the Indians, and the Indians had to climb the hill, out in the open, to defeat Custer. Robert wondered how many children were still being taught this biased story.

As children we were probably taught that all the American presidents were great, honorable and heroic men. Later, some may have discovered that they were not perfect but only human, like the rest of us. If you were a Catholic, you were also taught that the Pope is infallible and that his word is God's law. Historically, a council of Cardinals elected the Pope, and God supposedly directed them. If this was true, how could these men change any of the unchangeable laws of an unchangeable God? For instance, at one time it was against God's law to eat meat on Fridays. At a later time, the Church changed this law so that a Catholic could lawfully eat meat on Fridays. Similarly, the church hierarchy changed both the procedures of confession and of receiving Holy Communion. What was truth became a lie and what was wrong became right.

Science used to state that matter could neither be created nor destroyed. Formerly, this was a fundamental law known as *the law of conservation of matter*. Science has recently made important discoveries in the areas of atomic and nuclear physics. Today, scientists understand that matter can be completely transformed into energy by nuclear forces. As a result, this law has been changed to state that energy and matter are both conserved; neither can be created nor destroyed, but one can be transformed into the other. Whereas religions change their 'laws' because of ulterior motives, science only changes its laws when new evidence is discovered that disproves previous theories. The only motive of science is to find the truth.

During our childhood, we accepted many individuals as our authorities. Although these individuals may only have had superior knowledge to our own in one particular area, we often considered them to be an authority on *all* subjects.

In reality, most of them probably had no more knowledge of certain other subjects than any other individual. Both superiority and inferiority were illusions that stemmed from classifications that were always relative in nature. By the time Robert had enrolled in college, he realized that he could no longer blindly accept that which he had been taught as being factual. Robert needed to investigate and reason upon all of his acquired awareness.

All the information and data that we were forced to accept, or had unknowingly accepted, became fixed as awareness on our brain. The influence of this awareness was one factor that hindered the development of our reasoning ability. Information that we accepted from different authorities blocked our potential for reasoning. Believing at the time that we possessed true knowledge, we had no incentive to investigate or even to listen to new avenues of thought.

Jesus described those who just accepted the conventional opinions of others as the blind being lead by the blind. A great injunction of his was that man should seek the truth in order to be set free. How could a man search for truth? The answer wasn't to continually gather information and data on top of information and data. The more erroneous information we gathered, the more our awareness took on additional limitations.

When one has developed the ability to reason and discovers a truth, he becomes so excited about it that he wants to shout it from the rooftops. This was the case with the Greek philosopher, Archimedes, who discovered the principle of displacement while attempting to prove that his king's crown was made of gold. Archimedes was so excited by his new discovery that he forgot himself, jumped out of his bath and ran down the streets in the nude shouting at the top of his lungs, "Eureka, Eureka," meaning that he had solved the problem.

Knowingly or unknowingly, we have programmed or have permitted others to program our brain with limiting concepts. Unfortunately very few of us reason upon any of these limiting concepts. Only man has a brain that is capable of linking *percepts* and *recepts* together in order to form *concepts*. When these concepts are classified as good or bad, they become *programs*. It is these classifications of the concepts that have caused man to be 'kicked out' of the beautiful state of peace called the Garden of Eden. *Genesis* tells us that after man was sent forth from the garden, God placed two angels with fiery swords at its gates to guard the way back in. In order to get back into the garden, Adam and Eve were required to overcome the angels with the swords. These armed angels represent man's two methods of reasoning: deductive and inductive reasoning. Individuals must use these tools to evaluate any information they gain before it becomes concretely fixed within their awareness.

There is no real difference between an animal, a young child and a hypnotized subject, because awareness is impressed on their brains without them having any choice. Not one of these three has the ability to reason upon the information that is being impressed. Just as an animal trainer can teach a dog to be obedient, a child can be impressed with awareness that determines his likes, dislikes, religious beliefs, political convictions, and cultural conventions. As a child matures, he develops self-consciousness and the ability to reason. As a self-conscious individual, he now has the ability to choose what awareness will be impressed on his brain, to either accept or reject information. This process is called deductive reasoning.

Inductive reasoning, on the other hand, is referred to as the scientific method of investigation. This process starts with a question and a sincere desire to know the truth. It involves gathering data or information to answer the question, weighing, measuring and analyzing this information, coming to a conclusion based on the analysis, and finally testing and re-testing the conclusion.

Man's greatest gift is his ability to use both aspects of reasoning: inductive and deductive. After coming to a conclusion using inductive reasoning, it is necessary to reason deductively upon this conclusion so that it can be impressed upon the awareness. Therefore, both aspects of reasoning must be used in order to change the awareness within. This is the only way that man can remove himself from the limiting world of classifications, the world of self-consciousness. In order for Adam and Eve to re-enter the perfect peace of the Garden of Eden, they had to pass the test of reasoning represented by the two angels at the garden's gates. Only then could they eat of the Tree of Life, another tree in the garden.

Psychologists, and others who have investigated man's personality, have discovered that he has what they call a conscious, objective mind. This is the part of his personality that makes him conscious of his present environment. Further, this part of the mind is where reasoning takes place. The subconscious mind, on the other hand, only accepts awareness in the form of deductions. When this awareness is impressed with enough strength, the life expression of the individual will reflect it.

That which separates the conscious mind from the subconscious mind has been referred to as the *psychic barrier* or *psychic sensor*. The subconscious mind is that portion of the mind that contains all of past experiences and deductions since birth. Some researchers now believe that the subconscious mind also contains the awareness of all past creations, from the first subatomic particles to the highest of the animal kingdom.

All expressions of life below man are directed by instinct alone. These forms do not have the ability to alter this direction in any way; they do not have the ability to reason. Inherent in all matter is awareness that determines its life expression, from subatomic particles to man. Therefore, instinct or awareness is the director of subatomic particles, atoms, inorganic matter, plants and animals. From a theological viewpoint, this instinctive guidance is part of God or the 'voice of God'. God created man as a free moral agent, the first in all creation. Man has the ability to reason, to choose to follow or *not* follow this instinctive guidance.

Because of his unique ability to choose, man is able to direct his own expression of life. This ability is described in *The Book of Genesis*. God's first instructions to Adam were, "Of every tree of the garden thou mayest freely eat; But of the tree of the knowledge of good and evil, thou shalt not eat of it: for in the day that thou eatest thereof thou shalt surely die." Adam's instinctive guidance, therefore, would have been to follow the 'voice of God' and not eat of the tree of knowledge. However, *Adam chose* to disobey the instinctive guidance within him, and thus, became a self-conscious individual, separating himself from God. Other than man, none of God's creations had the freedom to obey or disobey His direction. Today, when an individual permits his environment to control him, he is not exercising his ability to reason inductively. Rather he is being guided by instinct and is only reasoning deductively.

In the Old Testament, there are many accounts of man being inclined to act without first weighing the influence of his awareness. The story of Abraham illustrates how man sometimes follows the customs of his tribe without first reasoning. It was customary in Abraham's tribe to sacrifice their most priceless possession to God. Without questioning, most of the tribe accepted this deduction and sacrificed their livestock as an offering to Him. Abraham expressed a higher consciousness than his fellow tribesmen did because he was developing his ability to reason. In addition, Abraham was very sincere in his devotion to the customs of the tribe relating to God.

Reasoning deductively, Abraham came to the conclusion that his livestock was not his most priceless possession, but that his son was. Therefore, he came to believe that to kill his son as a sacrifice was the right thing to do. Because that deduction became awareness within Abraham, he was inclined to act upon it. This is described in the biblical story as the voice of God instructing him to sacrifice his only son, Isaac. Abraham gathered the things he needed and prepared himself to perform the sacrifice. He was about to plunge the knife into his son's body when an angel of the Lord appeared before him and said, "...lay not thine hand upon the lad, neither do thou any thing unto him". The angel, sent from God, instructed Abraham to go against his inclination to slay his son. This is representative of Abraham recognizing a truth through the process of inductive reasoning. When reasoning inductively on a question, and after giving all solutions equal consideration, one is open to receive intuitive guidance.

This story also illustrates how one's environment influences his ability to reason. After the process of inductive reasoning is complete, and all information has been fully analyzed, one can gain intuitive guidance that one recognizes as a truth. However, if one does not complete the scientific method of investigation, and allows preconceived ideas or biases to influence his analysis, he is likely to come to a false conclusion. In this case, the subtle voice of intuitive guidance is drowned out by the louder voice of the inner environment, the awareness within.

In the story of *Genesis*, the Hebrews are portrayed as wanderers who roamed from place to place without any fixed roots. Thus, we may conclude that they were more or less a free people. The story continues by describing a great famine that forced them into Egypt, where a highly developed civilization existed. Because the Hebrews never completely accepted the Egyptian belief in many Gods, they were forced into slavery. During their enslavement, a Hebrew child, named Moses, was born into one of their families. The Pharaoh had commanded that all newborn Hebrew males be thrown into the river. In order to save the child from drowning, Moses' mother built a raft and set him adrift in the Nile River, having faith that God would rescue him. The Pharaoh's daughter found the child and raised him as her own to be an Egyptian prince.

At this time, the Pharaoh of Egypt had sole power to establish all customs and conventional opinions. As a prince of Egypt, Moses was educated in Egyptian law and history and soon began to question the conditions he saw around him. After recognizing the enslavement of the Hebrew people and the hardships that they were enduring, Moses began to question the customs and prejudices of the

Egyptians. From this starting point, Moses began the process of reasoning inductively upon the circumstances of Egypt at that time. His investigation led him to discover that he was actually born of a Hebrew family. Because he was not able to influence the authorities of Egypt to change their fixed ways, and since his life was in danger, he was forced to leave Egypt and enter the wilderness.

In going into the wilderness, Moses had rejected the customs and laws of his country. Moses' journey could be symbolic of man's renunciation of his personal, self-conscious awareness for a higher purpose. While in the wilderness, Moses suddenly became conscious that there was only one power that created everything and that ran it all. This awakening was symbolically portrayed in *The Book of Exodus*. Moses beheld the 'burning bush', and in that instant, became one with that power. He then realized that there was only one life and that the power was the director of that one life.

During this experience, Moses asked the burning bush by what name he could refer to this power when he spoke to his people. He received the reply, "...I am that I am". After the experience, Moses was able to hear the voice of God just as Abraham had heard it when he was about to slay his son. Moses was then directed to re-enter Egypt. This is symbolic of being directed to return to his self-conscious state. However, before he returned to this state, he was given the assignment of freeing his people from bondage and showing them the way to the Promised Land. After Moses had his experience and recognized the oneness of life, he was devoted to helping his fellow man to escape the bondage of limiting, self-conscious awareness. His assignment was to reveal to his people the oneness of all life.

There is a theory that, at that time, the Egyptians believed in two main gods: Isis and Ra. When Moses returned to his people, he referred to God as *Israel*, uniting the two gods into one God.

The story of *Exodus* described how God revealed His power to the Pharaoh through Moses. Moses then demanded the release of the Hebrews held in bondage. After the Pharaoh witnessed the power of God, he allowed the Israelites to leave Egypt. Moses led them through the wilderness, towards the Red Sea. In the meantime, God changed the Pharaoh's mind, and the Pharaoh ordered his army to pursue the Israelites and to stop them from escaping. Before the Israelites reached the sea, they looked back and saw the Egyptian army in pursuit. Being fearful for their lives, they began to regret their decision to follow Moses. In the process of renouncing their self-conscious lives, the Israelites were fearful of continuing on into the unknown life of freedom. At that moment, they wished that they could have remained in their old environment of enslavement.

The barrier preventing the Israelites from escaping and reaching the Promised Land was the Red Sea. Moses showed the way to freedom by parting the sea and leading the way. As the Egyptian army tried to follow, God commanded Moses to return the sea to its original state. All of the Egyptian army was drowned in the process. In order for one to have freedom from enslavement to limiting awareness, one must cross the barrier that separates the conscious from the subconscious mind.

By utilizing the principle of pleasure and pain in conjunction with the Ten Commandments, Moses tried but failed to bring freedom to the Israelites. The Ten Commandments only deterred them from expressing their animalistic natures, but continued to keep them at war within themselves. They were still not able to obtain peace nor were they able to reach the higher state of consciousness referred to as the Promised Land. As soon as their adverse conditions lessened and they became prosperous, the self-conscious nature characterized by greed, selfishness and jealousy overruled their reasoning ability. The Israelites lost the guidance of God and allowed priests and heads of state to have power and authority over them. They no longer recognized God as being the supreme and ultimate power of all life. As a result, they demanded that a king rule over them.

Moses tried to bring to man a way to reach God, a way to hear His 'voice', but he failed in his mission to bring the oneness of life to his people. He must not have realized that self-conscious classifications could never be overcome by the use of fear. By using fear to demand compliance to the Ten Commandments, Moses failed to give his people choice. As a result, the Israelites were not able to develop their reasoning ability so that they could reach the Promised Land on their own.

For hundreds of years, the authorities in the Israelite community abused the law and established customs and practices that eventually brought a greater enslavement to the people. For instance, the commandment of refraining from doing any work on the Sabbath day was taken to a ridiculous extreme. If a man's sheep fell into a well on the Sabbath day and was drowning, the owner could not act to save the sheep. The people were directed by these same authorities to make sacrifices to God and were told what they must eat and drink. The people were also told that they must blindly accept the authority of the temple priests, without question. Further, they were instructed that disobedience to these authorities would bring 'the wrath of God' down upon their heads. The fear of God served to control the animal or carnal nature in man to some degree, but it failed to give man the power to overcome 'the beast within'. In other words, they did not develop their ability to reason on the rules laid down by the authorities.

The teachings of Moses were limiting and, therefore, a greater teaching was needed in order to free man physically, mentally and spiritually. It was at this time that Jesus appeared upon the scene with a new philosophy of life. This new philosophy eventually upset and changed the established ways and beliefs of most of mankind.

Jesus rebuked those in authority for imposing rules and regulations to which even the authorities did not adhere. Whereas Moses used the pain aspect of the pain and pleasure principle to bring his teaching to the Israelites, Jesus used the constructive aspect of the law and taught love, not fear. He knew that the power of the priesthood was the most exacting, enslaving force in preventing the soul from becoming free. Jesus exposed the enslavement by the priesthood in revealing the true teachings from the Scriptures that later became the Old Testament. He taught that one should 'resist not evil', but that one should overcome it by applying the principle of love.

Jesus must have known that it was necessary for Moses to employ fear during that particular stage of man's evolution. At the same time, however, He must have also realized that fear did not free the soul from enslavement. He knew that His teaching could free man from the sin of ignorance. Jesus told the people that if they loved their mother, father or even themselves more than they loved Him, they were not worthy to be His disciples. Did this mean that they should not have loved their parents? It could not have meant that! Rather, it meant that they would only be able to discover the truth in His teachings to the degree that they were free of their limitations. If they allowed the classifications given to them by their mother, father and themselves, to interfere with and limit their reasoning ability, it would cloud their understanding of Jesus' teachings. The classifications clouded and colored their understanding of all new instruction.

Jesus said, "...if thine eye be evil, thy whole body shall be full of darkness. If therefore the light that is in thee be darkness, how great is that darkness!" This could mean that if one's awareness is so darkened by previous classifications, and he is not free of them, he cannot see God. Jesus also explained this in another way when He said, "Neither do men put new wine in old bottles, else the bottles break and the wine runneth out and the bottles perish, but they put new wine into new bottles and both are preserved." If the brain is filled with old classifications, it is like the old bottles; the old bottles will pollute the new wine or the new teaching. If one overcomes the old classifications he has acquired, he can obtain a greater understanding and a higher consciousness.

Jesus also said, "For whosoever will save his life shall lose it: and whosoever will lose his life for my sake shall find it". One's life expression, how he acts and reacts, is a reflection of his inner awareness. When one realizes that his limiting awareness has caused him to become a self-conscious being, then and only then will he realize that his view of life is an illusion. Only then will he be able to understand

and to impress into his awareness the truth of the teachings of Jesus. By doing this, he will rise above the self-conscious plane and enter into the higher consciousness of the one life.

Another statement by Jesus was, "Take no thought for your life, what ye shall eat, or what ye shall drink; nor yet for your body, what ye shall put on. Is not the life more than the meat, and the body than raiment?" In these statements, Jesus was presenting a method by which one could break up his self-conscious world. It is self-consciousness that separates us from God, the Father. Only when we overcome self-consciousness can we return to the Father within and be awakened to higher consciousness. Then, and only then, can we truly be the Sons of God.

Many Christians have a picture of Jesus standing on a mountain, giving a sermon to a large group of people. However, the New Testament describes the Sermon on the Mount differently: "And seeing the multitude, He went up into the mountain; and when He was set, his disciples came unto Him and He opened His mouth and taught them." Jesus must have known that in the multitude of people present, most of them thought only of themselves and only performed acts that would bring them personal pleasure. He also must have known that there were others who constantly vacillated between good and evil; sometimes they would try to give pleasure to others but, when their own existence appeared to be threatened, they would think only of themselves. However, among the multitude of people, there were a few who were trying to please the God of Moses by following the Ten Commandments to the best of their limited understanding. It was these few, and not the masses, who became the disciples of Jesus and to whom He taught the Sermon on the Mount.

The Hindu philosophy, as depicted in the *Baghavad Gita*, refers to these types of expressions as the three *Gunas*. The *Tamas Guna* represents the animal nature that men call evil. The *Rajas Guna* represents the self-serving nature, and the *Sattvas Guna* represents the spiritual nature that men call good. Jesus recognized these three distinct natures of man's expression. He was able to perceive the nature of each person gathered to hear the Sermon on the Mount and he chose to give instruction only to those of a Sattvas nature.

Jesus also said, "He that hath ears to hear, let him hear." Surely Jesus was not referring to physical ears. If the reader can grasp the deeper, esoteric meaning of this statement, he is one who has 'ears to hear'. Only one who is free from the influence of his own limiting awareness is able to understand the esoteric meanings of the teachings of Jesus.

> *Behold, a sower went forth to sow; And when he sowed, some seeds fell by the wayside, and the fowls came and devoured them up: Some fell upon stony places where they had not much earth: and forthwith they sprung up, because they had no deepness of earth; And when the sun was up they were scorched; and because they had no root, they withered away. And some fell among thorns; and the thorns sprung up and choked them: But others fell into good ground, and brought forth fruit, some an hundred fold, some sixty fold, some thirty fold.*

To the degree that one rises above his self-conscious awareness, he is able to understand the teachings from a higher level. Some would understand one hundred percent of the meanings, others sixty percent, and still others only thirty percent.

Throughout His teachings, Jesus constantly advised His followers to renounce their self-conscious awareness. It was this awareness that caused them to believe in many, separate lives. He taught that each individual, regardless of their level of consciousness, expressed only the *one* life, the Creative Essence. The followers of Jesus looked upon Him as God, a separate being, even though Jesus only taught and expressed the one life aspect.

Jesus said, "...I seek not mine own will, but the will of the Father which hath sent me." The miracles that Jesus performed were not intended to inspire His followers to glorify Him or to make Him God. Rather, the teachings and miracles came through his form, directly from God. Jesus stated this in many ways: "...He that believeth on me, the works that I do shall he do also; and greater works than these shall he do; because I go unto my Father"; and "...Why callest thou me good? there is none good but one, that is, God". How many understand these statements? Very few.

The followers of Jesus believed Him to be God, separate from man. According to them, he was not even born as all other men are! His Father, the spirit, impregnated a virgin who gave birth to God in form. These sentiments are still preached today in Christianity, and the name *Jesus Christ* is synonymous with divinity. The word *Christ* comes from the Greek word *Christos*, meaning anointed teacher. Therefore, it is possible that Christ could not even have been Jesus' literal name. Further, if Jesus' Father was not Joseph, then why does the Bible refer to the genealogy of Joseph in such detail? It may come as a surprise to some that the story of the virgin birth has been used by many religions to show that their founders were more than human. In order to establish their divine birthright to rule, emperors of Rome and other political rulers have used this same story.

Today, preachers of Christianity say that one needs only to believe that Jesus is divine to have everlasting life. Some even believe that in order to be born again, and 'be saved', they must only accept Jesus as their personal savior. Jesus need have known that his followers would consider Him to be divine, and so, He warned them of the consequences of just believing Him and not understanding the principles He taught.

> *Not every one that sayeth unto me, Lord, Lord, shall*
> *enter into the kingdom of heaven; but he that doeth the*
> *will of my Father which is in heaven. Many will say to me*
> *in that day, Lord, Lord, have we not prophesied in thy*
> *name? and in thy name have cast out devils? and in thy*
> *name done many wonderful works? And then will I*
> *profess unto them, I never knew you: depart from me,*
> *ye that work iniquity. Therefore whosoever heareth these*
> *sayings of mine, and doeth them, I will liken him unto*
> *a wise man which built his house upon a rock: And the*
> *rain descended, and the floods came, and the winds blew,*
> *and beat upon that house; and it fell not: for it was*
> *founded upon a rock. And every one that heareth these*
> *sayings of mine, and doeth them not, shall be likened*
> *unto a foolish man, which built his house upon the sand:*
> *And the rains descended, and the floods came, and the*
> *winds blew, and beat upon that house; and it fell: and*
> *great was the fall of it.*

After reviewing all the information he had gathered from reading, intensive studying and reflecting on the voice he had heard, Robert finally arrived at a conclusion using inductive reasoning. He concluded that there was one grand purpose for our existence. Using reason, we can evolve the awareness on our brain so that we can express, through our form, God at His highest potential. As a soul, it is our duty to manifest this potential. This is the purpose for our existence.

PART III

My Goal and My Destiny

MY GOAL AND MY DESTINY

Having discovered his purpose for existence, Robert realized that to divulge his findings, even to those nearest to him, would cause quite an upset. It would cause his friends and family emotional havoc and would result in their distrust and disbelief in him. However, he also realized that these reactions would be understandable because of the fixed, limiting awareness of others regarding religion. Robert knew that these reactions did not come from the soul, but rather, came from the limited awareness stored on the brain. He then understood that they would not be able to accept his conclusion until they had conducted similar research and analysis regarding their purpose for existence. Robert had no means to prove these conclusions to anyone else. He knew that, unless one was willing to evaluate and reason upon all his accepted views on life, he could never prove these conclusions to himself.

Robert didn't know what to do. How could he reach others who, like himself, were seeking answers? Was there some organization that was already teaching a similar philosophy of life, or would he have to search out and teach those seekers himself?

Robert had lived through the horror of two wars and had experienced many disturbing events. He was then comfortably employed and was living in a small community with his wife and three young sons. At this particular point in his life, although he had achieved most of the goals of the average, middle-class American, he was not satisfied. As a result, Robert decided to join the men's local Sunday Bible class. Every Sunday, while his two eldest sons were attending the Reform Church Sunday School, Robert attended his class.

One Sunday, the class received late notice that their regular instructor was unable to be present, and that he wouldn't be back for an entire month. The men in the class asked Robert if he would conduct the meetings for that period of time. He was asked to do this because he had often brought up some very salient points during their discussions of the Bible.

The fact that the men had asked Robert to lead them in their Bible studies did not prevent them from reacting to Robert's controversial points. Robert knew that they would react this way due to their limiting awareness but he continued his debates with the men in order for them to receive a better understanding of the lessons. Some of the men became very negative and distraught when debating crucial points, while others remained positive. A few even began to find fault with the manner in which Robert conducted the class. Robert then knew that anyone who attempted to get others with fixed beliefs to face the truth would confront a wall of bigotry.

Robert recalled what Jesus told his disciples when He sent them out to teach. Jesus must have realized they would have to confront the bigotry, belligerence and animosity of the masses. He advised them to, "Love your enemies", and, "Do good to them which hate you". Even when Jesus was being crucified, he said, "Father, forgive them, for they know not what they do." Earlier He also said to hate the 'evil one' because He must have realized that it is man's acquired, limiting awareness that expresses automatically as his life. He must also have realized that if man understood that he was enslaved to limiting awareness, he would eagerly strive to break the chains in order to change his expression of life; he would no longer need to automatically react to outside influences.

How many realize that when one expresses anger, it is due to his limiting, negative awareness, and does not originate from the soul? When anger is expressed from another, one should recognize that it is not necessary to respond in a similar manner; one can 'resist not evil'. Instead, one should first recognize this expression as originating from awareness. Then one can easily stand aside and use reason to neutralize the anger. When one can do this, he can add energy to the opposite of anger, which is patience. This expression of patience may then activate the awareness of patience in the angry person, thereby directing his attention to the way he is reacting. Even though the one expressing anger may still have that emotion, he may now become conscious of the other. In this way, the expression of patience can lower the strength of the anger within him. This is why, "A soft answer turneth away wrath."

Jesus said, "Love your enemies". Robert realized that many do not understand the principles behind this statement. In trying to explain these principles to the men in his study group, he drew a line on the board and wrote *love* on one side and *hate* on the other.

Love ——————————————— **Hate**

Below this, he drew another line with the word *hot* on the left and the word *cold* on the right.

Hot ——————————————— **Cold**

He attempted to give a concrete illustration of this principle by using the example of a cup of hot and a cup of cold coffee. Robert asked his class what they would do if they found their cup of coffee to be too hot and someone proceeded to pour boiling water into their cup. Robert asked them what they would think. Next, he described the opposite situation where the coffee was found to be cold and someone proceeded to put ice cubes in the cup. Again, Robert asked them what they would think.

An individual's first reaction might be to say, "You fool!" On the other hand, he might think that perhaps the person did not understand. He might then proceed to inform the other how to properly heat or cool one's coffee. The individual might say, "Instead of pouring hot water into a cup of coffee to cool it, the proper thing to do is to put ice into it, and in order to heat coffee that is too cool, the proper thing to do is to pour hot water into it."

Using this illustration, Robert explained to his students the principle that Jesus taught, "Love your enemies". Using the diagrams, he first explained that love and hate are only different degrees of emotion and that hot and cold are merely different degrees of temperature. Robert explained that in order to change one's expression from one extreme towards the middle, an opposite emotion would have to be visualized and given strength.

Add hate (less love) ⟶   ◀— *Add love (less hate)*
Love ——————————————————— **Hate**

Add cold (less hot) ⟶   ◀— *Add hot (less cold)*
Hot ——————————————————— **Cold**

Applying this principle, Robert further explained that in order to neutralize the emotion of hate, one must express love. This would reduce the hate being expressed from another. Likewise, if one was expressing love, and another came along who was expressing hate, unknowingly their love would be lowered toward hate. However, if one became conscious that he was a soul and a director of life, he would express love, knowing that love would raise the consciousness of one who was expressing even the greatest degree of hate.

It was evident that Jesus knew these principles and applied them in his own life. However, He was unable to convey these principles to his followers. Therefore, He told them to follow Him and live His teachings by faith. Even so, He told them that a time would come when the 'Spirit of truth' would take His teachings and make them understandable. Perhaps He foresaw the day when these principles would be proven by scientific means. Only then could the principles be taught to mankind and not be accepted by faith alone.

Through this kind of instruction in his Bible class, Robert attempted to correlate the findings of science with the teachings of theology. Even though he had upset the *status quo* of the group, he was successful in increasing class attendance. Robert wondered if this increase was due to genuine interest in finding the truth or was due to the intrigue of intellectual debate. At any rate, this increase in attendance did not go unnoticed! Robert was approached by several of the church leaders and was asked if he would agree to become a full time instructor of the Sunday School's teenage class. After giving the proposition some thought, Robert became elated at the prospect of teaching this particular age group. Knowing that these students were studying science in high school, he felt that he could give them more than conventional church history, doctrine and dogma. He could help the students to develop their own inductive reasoning so that they could find a correlation between science and theology for themselves.

Robert knew and taught that there was only one essence in the universe, which science called energy. He taught that energy expressed in the universe in three forms: as matter, awareness and force. Robert also taught that, from a theological view, there was only one God, but that God had three aspects: the Father, Son and Holy Spirit.

Through observation, man discovered that force was moving (kinetic) energy, and that it caused all matter to react. The behavior of matter as a force affected it was predictable, and as a result, the principles and laws governing this behavior were discovered. Science also proved that unless there was a difference of potential (stored up) energy in two bodies, there could not be a flow of kinetic energy between them.

For example, if the temperature in a room is already greater than that of the heat given off by a furnace, then the heat from the furnace will not affect the room temperature. This simple example shows that there cannot be a flow of energy unless there is a high potential to move from and a low potential to move to. Water never runs up hill.

Water exists in three different states: solid, liquid and gas. Ice has the lowest potential of energy, whereas steam has the highest amount of potential energy. By adding heat to ice, the ice changes into water, thus increasing its potential energy. Further, by adding additional heat, the water can be changed into steam, a yet higher potential. Any force that moves or changes matter must be kinetic energy.

All life, whether inanimate or animate, is the expression of matter activated by energy or force. Therefore, life is an expression of kinetic energy, and so, the same principles that govern *energy must* be the same principles that govern life. By learning the principles that direct energy, man can learn to direct his life expression.

After man discovered the principles of kinetic energy in the form of electricity, he was able to build mechanisms into forms that would produce a desired effect: the mechanism in an iron to produce heat, the mechanism in a light bulb to produce light, the mechanism in a radio to produce sound, etc. Built into these inventions was the awareness of producing heat, light and sound. Only a conscious creator had the ability to impress new awareness onto matter.

It is a scientific fact that for every effect, there must be a cause. Therefore, it is logical that if a man expresses anger, fear, worry or hate, there must be awareness built within his brain that causes his life to express as it does. However, within his brain is other awareness, and so, man also has the ability to express positive emotions such as faith, hope, love and kindness. Robert understood these principles and tried to bring them out in his classes.

As Robert continued to teach the class in this manner, the enthusiasm of the group increased with each passing week. There was seldom anyone absent from the class. Toward the end of the year, Robert and the other instructors were sent the usual end-of-the-year questionnaire. It was expected that the instructors would fill them out and return them to the Sunday School superintendent. One of the questions on the questionnaire read, "What do you feel your class should study during the forthcoming school year?" Having no idea of the impact it would have, he innocently wrote on the designated lines of his questionnaire, "Less church history, less church doctrine... and more of the teachings of Jesus." To his amazement, he was promptly and curtly informed that his services would not be needed in the next school year.

Because his students had made such great gains in their understanding, Robert was disappointed and angry at his dismissal. However, he learned a very important lesson from this experience. He realized that he was still capable of expressing negative emotions in the form of remorse, disappointment and anger. Until then, he thought that he had overcome the 'the beast within', only to find that there was limiting awareness yet to overcome within himself. He resolved to seek out the cause of this awareness and change its effects.

In making this resolution, something became crystal clear to Robert. At that moment, Robert knew his goal and his destiny in life! He saw it all so clearly! His goal and his destiny were to identify and neutralize the limiting awareness that had caused him pain and other negative emotions. After doing this, Robert knew that he could then replace that limiting awareness with a greater awareness of the oneness of all life. In so doing, the one energy, the one God, could flow through his form, giving him a greater consciousness and a greater life expression.

MY GOAL

Little did Robert realize how monumental the task was that he had set out to accomplish. However, he had a strong determination to find the truth. Robert's goal was to discover and eliminate all limiting awareness that made him a separate, self-conscious being, awareness that barred his union with the oneness of life. Robert wondered where to start the process of becoming conscious of all his limitations. Next, he wondered how he would change the awareness after he became conscious of these limitations. Once again, he decided that books held the answers; they were a good place to start.

Robert began his research by studying books on human behavior: the practices of psychoanalysis, psychotherapy and psychology. He extensively investigated two distinct methods of treating illness due to emotional disorders: psychotherapy and psychoanalysis.

Psychoanalysts believe that all of us have hidden, detrimental, associated concepts that, when triggered by an outside stimulus, are brought to our consciousness. Only then can we be in a position to reason on these concepts and to decide whether or not they have any basis in fact. Psychotherapists hold to another theory. They believe that if one accepts positive, beneficial suggestions regarding his problem, the new suggestions will neutralize or counteract the negative concepts operating within him.

Robert first researched some of the methods and techniques used by psychoanalysts. He discovered that there were two prominent psychoanalysts who had pioneered the modern form of the practice. An Austrian physician by the name of Sigmund Freud discovered that, by studying and analyzing his patients' dreams, he could uncover some of their subconscious wishes and desires. He theorized that these wishes and desires were being repressed, and therefore caused illness in the patient. Freud began to classify these desires and wishes by saying that they were instinctive urges trying to be expressed. One of his famous conclusions was that, "Repression is the cause and expression is the cure." It is evident that Freud's own experiences and environment influenced him in arriving at his conclusions. From reading Freud, Robert concluded that Freud's mother must have had a tremendous impact on the physician's life. She was loving, kind and very feminine. It is evident that he loved his mother dearly, and this must have influenced him to form his theory of *Eros*, the love instinct.

The other psychoanalyst, Carl Jung, disagreed with Freud's theory of Eros. In contrast to Freud's mother, Jung's mother was a strict, domineering Puritan who expressed very little love. Jung must not have accepted the Eros instinct theory because of his own awareness acquired from his mother. Instead, he explained human behavior in terms of a *collective unconscious* and its *archetypes*. Since that time, psychoanalysts have arrived at many different causative forces to account for aberrant behavior.

All psychoanalysts apply the same basic techniques to uncover the subconscious mind: dream analysis, free association and word association tests. There are other techniques that psychoanalysts employ, but the foundations of these other techniques are based on the three original methods. Even though the techniques have the same basis, analysis and interpretation of the results vary widely from one psychoanalyst to another, according to the theories that each have accepted.

In dream analysis, the patient is encouraged to relate his or her dreams to the analyst as completely as possible. The analyst then looks for clues from the dream and interprets the dream based upon the particular theory he accepts. If he is of the Freudian school, he usually looks for clues relating to sex. Analysts of other schools look for clues that relate to their particular theory and acquired awareness. After obtaining clues, the psychoanalysts use either free association or word association tests to gain further information.

Free association is based upon the spontaneous association of ideas. The psychoanalyst begins by getting the patient to relax, and while relaxed, the patient is encouraged to talk about anything that comes to mind. Although the patient may just ramble on and on, the analyst begins to direct the patient to talk about the experiences in his life. As the patient talks, the doctor analyzes these associated ideas according to his theories. Normally, the analyst begins by having the patient talk about his early childhood. The analyst looks for gaps in the patient's account of his early childhood, knowing that these may be indicative of repression. If repression is suspected, the analyst administers a word association test. He prepares a list of words to which the patient is to respond. Some words may cause a response from the patient such as physical reaction, hesitation, repetition, explanation or failing to respond at all to some words. All of these reactions furnish additional clues for the analyst to interpret. If one employs these methods on himself, it is called *self-analysis*. Some doctors believe that self-analysis can be very detrimental, and that it can lead to the development of guilt and self-condemnation.

The Catholic Church has its own form of dealing with guilt. Its method of removing guilt and sin is by way of confession. Sadly, the priests receiving the confessions often make the confessor feel guilty and responsible for their deeds by having them perform acts of penitence. This is contrary to the teaching of Jesus who said, "Father forgive them; for they know not what they do." Most children are punished for doing what their parents consider to be wrong. As a result, when a child does something which his parents, church or conventional opinion classifies as wrong, the child tries to hide such action from the authorities in his or her life.

Unless one can look upon his own expression of life as emanating from his computer-like brain, he will always feel responsible for his acts. One must realize that most people have never used their divine gift of inductive reasoning. Most have allowed others to program their awareness throughout their lives. If one can learn to use inductive reasoning, he can understand that his previous actions have come from his awareness that was programmed by someone else, and that he was not responsible. However, once he becomes conscious that his acts originate from his awareness and that he has the choice of whether or not to express those actions, only then does he become responsible.

Returning again to the subject of psychoanalysis, Robert arrived at some new conclusions. He realized that all acquired experiences were stored as awareness on the brain. Next, he realized that every stimulus that came through the five senses activated past awareness. Robert then reasoned that it was only necessary to receive a sense impression in order to bring up an entire chain of memories and associated classifications. Therefore, it was not necessary for anyone to go back into his early childhood in order to uncover limiting awareness that was affecting him. He could become conscious of his limiting awareness by observing his present life expression.

Robert further realized that people identified themselves as being their life expressions, and as a result, they found it almost impossible to alter their lives. Therefore, Robert began to practice 'standing aside' and observing his own reactions as if they were coming from another person. By doing this, he was able to objectively evaluate his reactions to certain stimuli. Robert then had a method to discover and analyze the limiting awareness that expressed as his life. In order to change his life expression, Robert knew that he had to neutralize his previous classifications of things, thoughts and acts. He wondered how he might do this.

Robert knew that he was enslaved to certain classifications and was mixed up in the opposites of good and bad. Upon investigating further, he gained an understanding that there is a law governing the principle of polarity called the law of relativity. The principle of polarity indicates that everything in the universe has opposite aspects. The law of relativity states that there are no absolutes in the universe, and that the opposite aspects of all things differ only in degree. Robert had not utilized this knowledge in the past. If he had, he could have related every one of his negative experiences to something worse, and then he could have classified all his experiences as positive. He could only accomplish this task through an understanding of the law of relativity. Robert remembered a saying that was a good illustration of relativity: "I bemoaned my fate because I had no shoes, until I met a man who had no feet!" Having become conscious that he was not his thoughts, but that he was the observer of those thoughts, Robert could see all life as God saw it; he could call everything *good.*

Robert next began his investigation into the field of psychotherapy. Whereas psychoanalysts delve into the past experiences of the patient, psychotherapists attempt to impress positive suggestions on top of existing awareness. The doctor attempts to get the patient to listen to constructive suggestions. Their theory is that if these new suggestions are impressed into the subconscious as awareness, they will cause the patient to express them instead of their old awareness.

There are two main techniques that are used to impress the new suggestions into the patient's awareness. One method employed by the therapist is that of *agreement.* By his actions and tone of voice, the therapist must conduct himself in such a way as to be an authority to his patient, in order for the suggestions to be accepted. When the therapist is the authority, everything that is said will be impressed into the patient's subconscious, unless the suggestion stimulates some contradictory awareness. Any suggestion that is impressed will incline the patient to carry it out and express life differently.

The other method employed by many therapists is to *fascinate* the patient. This method is normally used in the art of hypnosis. The patient is often told to stare at an object that is held above his eve-level. The longer he stares at the object, the more tired his eyes become. The therapist then amplifies this reaction by continually repeating words or phrases relating to sleepiness, drowsiness or tiredness. When the suggestion has enough strength, it will cause the patient's body to become totally relaxed. At this time, like in normal sleep, the patient's reasoning faculty becomes dormant. After the patient has entered into this state, the therapist can successfully impress new awareness in the patient's subconscious. The awareness that is impressed will incline the patient to carry out the new, positive suggestions.

The first stage in the process of becoming a hypnotized subject is called *lethargy*. Suppose, for an example, while the subject is in this state, the operator tells him that he will be given a high ball. The operator holds a glass of water while saying, "This is a high ball, a high ball, a high ball, a high ball." When he feels that the subject has sufficiently accepted the concept that the glass actually contains a high ball, he hands the glass to the subject and repeats the same words. The operator then tells the subject to tip the glass and drink the high ball down. Since the subject is, in his own mind, drinking alcohol, and because he has previous experience with being intoxicated, he begins to feel and act inebriated.

In the past, and still today, many hypnotic operators believe that they possess some mystical power. The churches even believed that these operators had a power that originated from the devil. At one time, the medical profession also had a negative attitude concerning hypnosis. Today, however, the medical profession embraces hypnosis to the extent that they claim to be the only authorities on it. They have even attempted to have laws passed forbidding the practice of hypnosis by anyone other than medical practitioners.

Perhaps neither the medical profession nor the churches know that a person cannot be hypnotized with a suggestion that goes contrary to that person's morals. If a subject is given a suggestion that goes contrary to his previous

awareness, the patient becomes conscious of his old awareness. This causes two alternate inclinations to come to consciousness in the subject. The patient must awaken in order
to make a choice between the two alternatives. Therefore,
a hypnotized subject will not do anything that goes against
his moral code. The inebriated subject in the above
example had no difficulty accepting the suggestion of
becoming intoxicated because getting drunk was not
against his moral code.

If one understands the principles underlying hypnosis and
suggestion, one would realize the ridiculousness of the law
the medical doctors were trying to pass. If the law had been
passed, it would have forbidden every preacher, teacher,
salesman and leader from practicing his or her profession!
Knowingly or unknowingly, they employ hypnotic principles every day of their professional lives. Every form of
advertising, promotion and selling is based upon the application of hypnotic principles.

After uncovering these principles, Robert knew that all his
previous, acquired awareness was nothing more than post-
hypnotic suggestions implanted by others. With this knowledge, he then understood what Jesus meant when He
referred to souls as being dead or asleep. Jesus must have
known that most individuals did not reason upon these suggestions and, therefore, blindly followed them.

Having arrived at this new understanding, Robert had the
working tools to continue the quest of achieving his goal.
He then recalled the story of how Francis Bacon, after in-
depth research at many universities, became obsessed with
finding the ultimate truth. After years of seeking, Bacon
decided that it was necessary to analyze all the knowledge

he had ever gained and to classify it as fact, theory or fantasy. As Bacon examined all his acquired awareness, he began to break up its limiting classifications. As a result, his perception and conception of the world was forever changed.

Robert resolved to follow the same method Bacon had used. Like Bacon, Robert was driven by some inner force to continue his search. Today, a greater number of people are also examining their own awareness and are classifying it as fact, theory or fantasy. As a result, accepted customs and conventions around the world are being changed or eliminated. Beliefs are being shattered, governments are crumbling, people are losing faith in their religions, and economic and financial institutions are in chaos. Some look upon these changes as being signs of an approaching apocalypse.

Robert wondered about these signs and decided to re-read *The Book of Revelation*. After contemplating what he had read, he realized that the world that was to be destroyed was the self-conscious world of awareness. Just as Francis Bacon had destroyed his conceptual world, so too was mankind beginning to free itself from its self-conscious awareness. It seemed logical to Robert that if one could destroy his own self-conscious world, then and only then would 'the breath of life', the 'Son of God', the *soul*, awaken within him. Using the laws of energy that are the laws of life, Robert began to destroy the self-conscious world within him. As he did, he gained more peace and a greater understanding of *life* and *consciousness*.

A MYSTICAL EXPERIENCE

Robert's position as a Sunday School teacher had been terminated abruptly. This did not stop Robert, however, from continuing his search for the truth, and so he turned his attention to other activities in his spare time. As a result of his new activities, he became closely acquainted with some of the men in the community who were Masons. He and his wife were invited to various social affairs, among which were social activities hosted by members of the Masonic Lodge. He continued to enjoy the company of his Masonic friends and finally, one day, he asked one of them how he might become a member of their organization.

After he became a member and had met all the requirements of First and Second Degree Masonry, Robert became a Master Mason. One of the vows he made was to never reveal the Ancient Secrets of Masonry. He studied the instruction he had received, worked his way up through the chairs of his lodge, and became a Thirty-second Degree Mason.

Robert took his study of Masonry just as seriously as he had taken his other studies. He attended his Lodge meetings regularly and even became an instructor of new applicants. He still had no idea what these ancient secrets were and where he could find them. One Saturday evening, the ladies of The Eastern Star were holding their annual banquet meeting for the Lodge. A professor from Rutgers University had been invited to give a lecture and a demonstration on clinical hypnosis.

During the war, Robert had taken some advanced courses at Rutgers while stationed at a nearby army post. When the professor asked for volunteers for his demonstration, Robert felt a sense of obligation to assist due to his previous association with the university. Never having been a hypnotic subject before, Robert was surprised to find that he 'went down' quite easily. This experience later led to an event that was to have a profound influence on Robert's life.

After the demonstration by the professor, a fellow Lodge member's brother-in-law, who was a chiropractor, asked Robert if he was interested in knowing more about hypnosis and related subjects. Robert replied that he was not especially interested, but his friend persisted by inviting Robert to attend a lecture with him and his brother-in-law in New York City.

"What's it all about?" asked Robert.

"Well," said the chiropractor, "to tell you the truth, I really don't know. But I'll tell you what; if it isn't worth our while, we can always leave and have a night out on the town." Robert agreed to go.

After they arrived at the lecture, they discovered that most of those in attendance were chiropractors. They stayed to listen to the entire lecture, even though it was poorly presented. For some unknown reason, the three of them enrolled in the class that was to be held the following weekend.

This was Robert's introduction to the philosophy known as Concept Therapy. The following weekend, Robert took his seat in the class, wondering what in the world was going to be presented that would take three days of instruction. As the class progressed, Robert was most interested in the attempt that was made to correlate science and theology. While sitting and listening, Robert became more and more amazed to learn that someone else had arrived at many of the same conclusions that he had. The thrill he felt at discovering this was beyond description. For Robert, this feeling couldn't be contained. He couldn't wait to find out as much as possible about the founder of Concept Therapy, a man named Dr. Thurman Fleet. Robert wasted no time during the class breaks in asking the instructor questions about Dr. Fleet. The instructor told Robert some very interesting stories about the founder. In particular, he told Robert that Fleet had had a cosmic illumination in 1931. As a result of this experience, Fleet had devoted his life to helping mankind through teaching the philosophy of Concept Therapy. Upon hearing this story, Robert couldn't wait to meet him.

It wasn't until much later, however, that Robert got the chance to meet Dr. Fleet. One year later, he finally received a notice that Dr. Fleet was coming into the area to teach a special course in Middletown, New York. By this time, Robert had purchased several audio tapes by Dr. Fleet. From the tone of the voice on the tapes, Robert had developed a mental picture of the doctor. He pictured a long, tall Texan, about the size of John Wayne.

On the day Fleet was to arrive, Robert drove his family to Middletown to attend the class. Upon entering the classroom, they were greeted by fellow classmates with the usual hellos and handshakes. One of the handshakes exchanged with Robert was a particularly weak, fishy one by a rather short gentleman. Robert was looking over the heads of all those present, trying to catch sight of the big, tall Texan. Robert was not able to locate anyone in view who even remotely resembled John Wayne. Consequently, not wanting to appear too eager, Robert nonchalantly approached an instructor he knew and asked him to point out Dr. Fleet. The instructor led Robert across the room, back to the man at the classroom entrance. Robert was shocked to discover that the man the instructor led him to was the short man with the weak handshake. Unable to contain his surprise, Robert blurted out, "You mean this is Dr. Fleet?"

"Yes!" boomed the small man confronting him, "I'm Fleet."

Soon after, Fleet began teaching the class. At one point during the presentation, Robert was again shocked by Fleet's performance. Fleet jumped up and down on the platform, made loud bugle-like sounds, and declared that he was Gabriel who had come to announce the end of the world. After this event, Dr. Fleet settled down to a less boisterous method of instruction, and Robert began to do some serious thinking about all the events that had taken place that day.

Why the Gabriel act? Why the weak handshake? Why all of the other antics? Robert knew that Fleet was acting this way for a particular reason. Fleet may have acted the fool, but he was far from being one! The Concept Therapy text proved to Robert that this man had something beyond the comprehension of most. So why these shenanigans?

As Dr. Fleet continued to teach, it dawned on Robert that the man was trying everything in the book to get his students to reason upon his actions. Robert thought that if the Gabriel act and the weak handshake didn't do it, God himself couldn't do it either. It was becoming clear to Robert that he was listening to a master. During the course of the class, Robert spoke to Dr. Fleet on several occasions and started to recognize him as a master. During one of these occasions, Robert asked Fleet if he would speak with his son, Robert Junior, who was having difficulty with his studies in school.

During a class break when everyone was socializing, Dr. Fleet took Robert Junior aside. He removed a five-dollar bill from his pocket and playfully showed it to the boy. "Son", he said, "I'm going to put this money in my right hand and close my fist over it. I'm going to tell myself that my fist cannot be opened. Now, if you can get me to open my hand, you can have the money." By that time, Dr. Fleet had captured Robert Junior's undivided attention. The boy watched attentively as Fleet's hand tightly closed around the bill. Robert Junior started saying over and over, "You can open your hand, you can open your hand, you can open your hand."

By this time, a small audience had gathered around them, but the crowd went unnoticed by the boy. His eyes were glued on Dr. Fleet's fist as he kept repeating, "You can open your hand." Finally, Dr. Fleet started to loosen his grip on the five-dollar bill. At the precise psychological moment, when his hand was fully opened, he thrust the bill out towards the boy and said, "...and Robert, you can study too!"

After this, Fleet went back to the podium and announced to the class that Robert Junior would never again have difficulties in school. Further, he said that when his family moved to the Concept Therapy headquarters, Robert Junior would be the keeper of the horses. The whole Casper family was dumbfounded. They were not thinking of making a move, especially not to the Concept Therapy Institute in Texas – otherwise known as the *ranch*. They soon discovered, however, that Fleet's statement turned out to be true.

Within a matter of months, Robert's wife, Jane, developed some health problems. As a result, the Casper family decided to move to the ranch so that Jane could attend the three-month program at the ranch's health clinic. During this temporary stay, Robert became quite familiar with the ranch's 318-acre property. He also got to know many of the residents and officers of the Concept Therapy Institute. His visit provided the opportunity to get together with others at the ranch for many stimulating, philosophical discussions.

After having had some long discussions with Dr. Fleet, rumors began to circulate at the ranch that Robert was going to be a teacher of Concept Therapy. When Robert asked other residents how they knew he was going to teach, they all said that Fleet had told them so. At that time, Robert had not even considered teaching. However, after he returned home, Robert eventually decided that he wanted to teach Concept Therapy. This was an important step towards a future event that forever altered the direction of his life.

For two years, Robert faithfully studied and applied the teachings of Concept Therapy and taught classes around the country, realizing that he had been given a roadmap of life. He realized that the teachings were a means of bringing freedom to himself and to those in his midst. Living the teachings allowed him to identify and eliminate the limiting awareness that enslaved him physically, mentally and spiritually. Robert had found a means to achieve his goal and destiny.

During these two years, Robert continued to break up concepts that caused him to be self-conscious. He continued to read many books in order to investigate metaphysical teachings. From Robert's state of higher consciousness, he could see that all these metaphysical and occult schools exalted self-consciousness by promising supernormal powers to their followers.

From his understanding of the human personality, Robert could see that these promises lead to another type of enslavement. Some of these schools taught that one must continually repeat sounds like *aum* and meditate in order to still the mind. Robert understood that by repeating a sound that was not associated with anything in the awareness, nothing would come to consciousness. In this state, one would experience relaxation of the body and emotional rest. However, would this technique make the individual conscious of his limiting awareness? Robert knew that it wouldn't! For a brief period while concentrating on such a sound, an individual could escape from pain experienced in third dimensional consciousness, just as one could briefly escape with the use of drugs or alcohol. Robert did not want to become unconscious of that which had been programmed in his awareness. Rather, it was his objective to bring this limiting awareness to consciousness so that he could unravel his self-conscious ego.

By observing and contemplating the vast variety of life, Robert reaffirmed that there must be only one source to it, with many expressions. No longer was his contemplating a mere intellectual exercise. Robert developed a 'knowingness' and a consciousness that there was only one life. From that time on, he knew that he was the soul, observing all of his experiences from this perspective. It then became easier for Robert, as an objective observer, to investigate his awareness without becoming emotionally involved with it. His ability to think and evaluate his awareness increased immensely.

One day, Robert was pondering on the esoteric meaning of the story of Christ's crucifixion. He wondered about the significance of Christ being crucified between the good thief and the bad thief. Why was Christ in the middle, between the two thieves? What was the esoteric meaning of a *good* thief? It was then that Robert became conscious of a change that was taking place within his body. It seemed to Robert that his body was becoming less dense and was radiating a purplish-blue light. A quietness surrounded him and he felt as if he were dissolving into space. Everything began to fade away from Robert's view and he felt as if he were leaving his body. He soon became conscious that his form was becoming translucent and was glowing with an ever-increasing brilliance. Robert then observed what appeared to be a new being that was expressing through the body he used to occupy. The more Robert continued to observe, the more this being came into existence. Finally, it began to speak to him.

It said, "You who have inhabited this form are not real. You are only a reflection of my limited expression through that form. I alone exist. Expressing in that form, I created an illusion that you believed was real, and because you identified with it, you thought that you were a separate and distinct personality. What you are now observing is my glory as it could be expressed in a form that was free and had perfected itself. You, with your limited understanding, would call this expression a son of the highest or God in form. Now observe me in all nature, and with my inner sight awakened in your form, you will see my light in all you observe and you will feel me, which is yourself, in all forms."

At that moment, Robert became conscious of being in the trees, in the leaves, in the fly that landed on his arm, and in the grass he stood upon. A sense of immortality filled his being. He was in everything and he was also the observer of everything. Robert had no words that could describe this state of consciousness. While Robert was in this state, there was no sense of time, but sometime later he was given instructions and was also given an assignment that he was to carry out. Robert then beheld a vision. It was the manifestation of this vision that was the destiny he was to follow.

For two days following this initial experience, Robert felt as if he were living in two worlds: the external, third dimensional world and the inner world of existence that he had never before fully experienced. On the second evening, after he had eaten dinner, Robert went down to the recreation room in his house. At that time, he was inclined to take a tape recorder with him and to begin recording. Robert sat down in a chair and then began to feel that he was fading away. It was the same sensation that he had experienced the day before. Shortly after, he began to receive more instruction. While Robert was experiencing the instruction in the form of images, the awareness on his brain was activated by the same energy. At the same time, Robert's form began speaking, relating the words associated with the awareness that had been activated by the images. The following instruction was recorded on the tape.

"You have now reached the point in understanding and in consciousness where we are ready to give you instruction and guide you into higher wisdom. Today you have felt, from time to time, that you were leaving your body and being conscious of a feeling that you are one with others or can know what they are thinking.

You also have thought that you had some special powers. You could mentally have others carry out orders, such as, 'Get up from your chair and go outside.' You looked at a dog that was barking and you mentally had him stop barking and lay down. You thought that you were directing that animal to respond from your thinking. Last night you knew Al Ross had a pain in his left leg. You touched it, and the pain was gone. Again, you thought you had some power and now you must know how all these things happen. First, let us bring you back to Sunday when you experienced that you were alone in the class and there was no one else in the room. You felt as though you could control and direct energy, and also that you were only one.

Remember when you returned home, you also found yourself listening as you now are doing. We asked you that night to read the Gita, at various places. You had purchased the Gita before and you know that you went through the Gita and read only those things we talked about. The next day we know you underlined most of those sayings in your book. For instance, 'Thou knoweth that there is nothing in the universe but me'. You are me, and it is you who now speaks through the form you occupy. Yes, it is difficult to fully understand and comprehend when I ask you to speak to me and you are listening as if I am different from you. But it is so difficult when you and I exist as separate forms. It is the same as you, a conscious expression, have learned about energy and matter. The matter is energy, but all conscious forms of matter cannot comprehend that they are all one essence, energy. As you listen, it is your teaching. As you listen, it is you teaching you, from the oneness of it all, which you now know as part of yourself. Consider us coming from us on this higher level of consciousness.

I ask. I, as we know in matter form, must accept instructions as coming from other individuals. That being so, then I, as you, can name us as the masters. I will give you another example that will awaken within you a realization. There is light, but when that light passes through matter, it becomes different colors, as you know. I ask you, 'Are these colors real and separate from the light?' If they were conscious, they could believe that they were a separate creation, a separate creation in form. My brother, you are the color but you have now become the light.

Look at these forms that I occupy and that obey your commands. They could consider that you also were a color and had power over them. It is you in those forms that carry out the action. That gross material plane will cause you to become, once again, a separate color, but you will know that you are the light. It is you, in those forms, that gave the order to move or speak. It is you that is speaking to you now. It is difficult to comprehend that you are all that exists. So you must recognize this as a great truth. From now on, your symbol will be the rainbow, and you must enter into a new existence.

When you return, and this is understood, you will gather other expressions of you who are lost and missing, and you will, as a separate being, teach them slowly how they too can become you. You will seek out those others. You cannot enslave them. You cannot teach them separateness, but you must find the way to reveal to them the oneness of you. We are speaking of you as if we were individuals, separated, but we are all you.

Think on this and know that all you experience is coming because of you. In a few days, by your standard, you will receive understanding of your mission in that form you occupy, as being separated from you. You must build a place where all expressions of you can live and experience the wonders of your creation. It has been necessary for you to create separateness in form, just as the light changes the colors of the rainbow. So, you have impressed in matter different expressions of you who are separated. Now, you must bring those colors into the light. We know that you are recording this, but you will not have any more recordings made. For it will not help you in your form. But it may be that this tape will be necessary for you, in form, to help those who are seeking this same oneness. The time will come when instructions will be expressed from your form, informing other expressions of you to hear this recording. But until then, this must not be played. Now we want you to turn the machine off so that we can tell you more about your new existence."

It was impossible for Robert to express in words what took place when he entered into *uniconsciousness.* This entire experience lasted for ten days, and at the end of it, Robert had a sensation of falling from a great height and landing with a tremendous weight. He had returned to his normal state of consciousness. After his indescribable experience, Robert wondered how he could ever relate this experience to others. Robert even wondered for a brief period of time if he were insane. After contemplating his experience for some time, he was convinced that his goal was to perfect his limited expression and carry out the assignment he had been given. By perfecting his limited expression, Robert could help the light in all self-conscious beings shine brighter, so that they too could become conscious of the divine destiny and feel divine love and divine essence within themselves. Robert realized further that he could only accomplish this magnificent goal by carrying out the assignment that he had been given. His assignment consisted of three parts:

1. To manifest 'the vision' on the physical plane

2. To write a book telling how he had found his path to truth

3. To teach a philosophy of the *one life*

After this experience, Robert knew for certain that he understood what Dr. Fleet had been teaching. He knew that Dr. Fleet's aim was to slowly raise the consciousness of individuals from the self-conscious level to that of *uniconsciousness*. This realization caused Robert to make a vital decision. More accurately, a decision was made for him. It was decided that he would give up his employment, leave his beautiful new home, move to Texas and teach Concept Therapy full-time.

The day before the Caspers were to leave for the ranch they received a phone call from Dr. Fleet informing them of a "real nice" cottage that he had secured for them at a very nominal fee of only fifty dollars a month. The cottage had, as an added feature, a "real nice" screened-in porch. He also said that the owner seldom rented the cottage, but since the Caspers were coming to Texas as full-time instructors, they could have it. Robert couldn't recall the cottage that Dr. Fleet was describing, but because the ranch was so large, he thought that maybe he had just overlooked it. The last time they had visited the ranch, Jane had not seen any house that she particularly liked. At any rate, he felt that the house Dr. Fleet had arranged would be fine until he could build the house that he had promised his wife.

It was a Sunday afternoon when the Casper family pulled into the ranch. In the car was Robert, his wife, three boys, a cat named Cosmos, and behind the car was a loaded U-Haul trailer. Dr. and Mrs. Fleet were there to greet them, and after the usual formalities and a little visit, Dr. Fleet asked one of the staff to show the Caspers to their new home. Dr. Fleet said that it had been cleaned up and was ready to be moved into.

There weren't any words in the English language that could have described their surprise and amazement when the Caspers finally saw the cottage. They were shocked, dumbfounded and flabbergasted. Before them stood an old, broken down shack with a porch surrounded by a screen full of holes! As they slowly walked through the front door, they saw all kinds of bugs, including daddy-long-leg spiders climbing all over the walls! Then they saw the shower! When they turned it on, the water came up in the kitchen sink, creating a disgusting mess.

Jane's instant reaction was to 'turn heel' and leave at once. It took a lot of persuasion before Robert could calm his wife down to the point where he could even reason with her. He kept insisting that this was just Fleet's test to see what they would do. Robert insisted that they couldn't leave. Finally, after having convinced her to stay, they started to make themselves as comfortable as possible for their first night. This took a little forethought and quite a bit of ingenuity. They had never lived in an eighteen by twenty-foot room before and decisions had to be made before nightfall.

They had brought a roll of metal screen that they could fasten over the inside doorway that lead to the porch. They carted out all the old furniture that was sitting around into the yard and brought in some of their own. That night, Robert and two of the boys slept in the station wagon. They decided that they would straighten the whole mess out in the morning.

The next morning, they moved their couches, chairs, tables, beds, dressers and boxes into the tiny shack. Later that morning, there was a knock on the door. It was Dr. and Mrs. Thurman Fleet coming to pay a visit. All she needed was one step inside the shack and Mrs. Fleet exclaimed, "Thurman! How in the world could you do such a thing to these nice young people?" Dr. Fleet ignored his wife's protest and began stepping over boxes and furniture, looking for a place to sit down. Once settled, Dr. Fleet asked for an ashtray because he didn't want to get ashes on the "nice clean floor."

All this might have seemed ludicrous and unbelievable to Robert if he hadn't been familiar with Fleet's way of teaching. Most anyone else would have left in disgust, but Robert knew what the lesson was in this situation. Dr. Fleet was teaching them the law of relativity. Why? Prior to moving, Jane had made it known to Fleet that none of the houses at the ranch were suitable for her and her family. At the time, she was comparing the houses at the ranch to the beautiful, new home they had just left. After this experience, however, any other house on the ranch would have seemed luxurious in comparison to the shack. Fleet knew that after Jane had lived in the shack for even a brief period of time, it wouldn't take her long to adjust to any other house on the ranch and be happy.

Eventually, the Caspers did move into another house and stayed there for four years. During these four years, the Caspers had many memorable experiences. However, there was one major incident that none of them ever forgot.

It involved Robert Junior, who had previously been told by Dr. Fleet that he would be the keeper of the horses. When the Caspers first moved to the ranch, there were no horses. It wasn't long, however, before Robert was approached by one of Fleet's relatives about buying a burro. Robert bought the burro and the boys named it "Dusty". Neither Robert nor the boys had ever had any experience with burros, but they were told that burros were very inexpensive to keep as they lived mostly off the land.

Several days later, Dr. Fleet drove up to the Caspers' house and asked Robert to go out to the corral with him to examine Dusty. After the examination, Dr. Fleet's diagnosis was that Dusty was in poor condition due to malnutrition. Because of this, Dr. Fleet prescribed a mixture of oats, rye, sugar and salt to be fed to Dusty every morning. Following Dr. Fleet's orders, Robert and Robert Junior went out to the corral early each morning to feed Dusty the mixture that would once again make him whole. A few days after they started feeding the burro this diet, Calvin Wright, Dr. Fleet's brother-in-law, came rushing into the Casper home. He shouted, "Dusty and her colt are lying out in the field and their stomachs are bloated to high heaven! Robert, you better go get a vet quick!"

As he ran out the door and jumped in his car, Robert yelled back and told Calvin to call the vet. He was going to take a look at Dusty and Zero. Robert found both animals just as Cal had described, all sprawled out and miserable. He certainly didn't want Fleet to come driving up and see a sight like this! In desperation, he reached down, picked up the tails of both burros, one in each hand. He then looked over at two Mexican ranch workers, sitting nearby on the corral fence, and yelled, "Look out boys, cause if Dr. Fleet's teaching works, when I yank these tails, you'll wish you were a mile down the road from here!" With that, Robert gave one great big yank, saying to himself, "Perfect and normal, perfect and normal, perfect and normal." All of a sudden, Robert began to hear a low, rumbling noise. It grew louder and louder until finally all hell broke loose! There lay Dusty and Zero deflated and still passing gas.

After this episode, Robert Junior had his fill of tending to burros; he wanted a horse. Upon returning home from teaching a class one afternoon, Robert and Jane were surprised to see Robert Junior riding around the ranch on a horse. Robert Junior later explained to them that it belonged to a classmate's father who wanted to sell it. The father would take fifty dollars down and Robert Junior could work for him during the summer to pay off the balance of thirty-five dollars. Since he had the initial fifty dollars saved from his paper route back east, and was willing to work off the balance during the summer, Robert gave his consent; Robbie could have the horse.

One morning about a month later, Robert and Jane spent the day in nearby San Antonio. Before returning to the ranch, they dropped in to visit Dr. Fleet at his home. As soon as they walked in, Dr. Fleet asked them if they knew what had happened at the ranch. "No we don't," they replied. They said that they had been away all day and hadn't heard anything. Dr. Fleet proceeded to tell them that some of the residents at the ranch had reported Robert Junior to the Society for the Protection of Animals. They reported that the boy had been mistreating his horse. Some ranch residents had signed affidavits stating their complaints, and the Caspers had been subpoenaed to appear in court the next day. Dr. Fleet said that the judge had called him on the matter and that he had told the judge that he, himself, had no knowledge of the situation. "Now what?" thought the Caspers. It couldn't be true! They knew that Robert Junior took excellent care of the horse and loved it dearly.

The next afternoon Robert, Jane and Robert Junior drove to the courthouse to see the judge. They related to the judge the facts regarding Robert Junior's care of the horse. They suggested that there had been some misunderstanding. "Perhaps someone saw Robert Junior attempting to train the horse and mistook what they saw as some kind of mistreatment," said Robert.

After a short period of interrogation and after listening to the boy's account of his care of the horse, the judge let him go with a mild warning. As they left the courthouse and were on the way to their car, they saw Dr. Fleet driving up to the building. Fleet said he thought he would drop by to see how things were going and that it was too bad that things had turned out this way. Turning to Robert Junior, Fleet proceeded to tell him that no one at the ranch cared for the likes of him at all. Shocked and hurt, the Caspers got in their car and drove home.

That night, despite the recent hassle, Robert and Jane attended the weekly ranch meeting. They walked in without saying a word about the day's events and found two empty seats right next to two of Robbie's prime accusers. Needless to say, after fidgeting and squirming in their seats for a while, the two accusers got up and left. When Robert and Jane got home from the meeting, they found that Robert Junior was still awake and was still just as disturbed as they were.

Robert Junior said, "Dad, I don't want to hurt anyone here on the ranch. Do you think that if I take the horse back to Mr. Smith he will return my money?" Taken aback for a minute, Robert looked at his son with pride and deep admiration, seeing within him a good and strong character.

"Son," he said, "even though you may not realize it, you have now truly become 'the keeper of the horses'." That same night, at Robbie's insistence, Robert followed him in the car as he rode the horse nine miles to the Smith ranch. They arrived some time after midnight. Mr. Smith, who had waited up for them, came out with a check and handed it to Robbie in exchange for the returned horse.

Robert asked Mr. Smith if he would mind examining the horse before they left. Mr. Smith took the horse into the stable where he could get a closer look at it. After having checked him over thoroughly, Mr. Smith came back out and told them that the horse was in excellent condition. "In fact," he said, "he's in better condition than when I sold him to you." Robert then asked Mr. Smith if he would please contact both the judge and Dr. Thurman Fleet and inform each of them of the horse's condition. Mr. Smith said that he knew Dr. Fleet very well and that he would be sure to inform both him and the judge in the morning.

Robert wanted the report on the horse to be known because he had come to the conclusion that this whole affair had been planned and executed in order to test the Caspers again. However, what he couldn't understand was why those who had been asked to take part in the hoax never once questioned why they had been chosen by Fleet to do so.

Robert's strong suspicions were confirmed one day near the end of their fourth year at the ranch. Dr. Fleet called Robert into his office and apologized to him in front of both the Concept Therapy Institute's lawyer and its auditor. Fleet said that ever since the Caspers had moved to the ranch, he had been trying to get them to leave. Because of their dedication, however, they had refused to leave under any circumstances.

What was it that had caused the Caspers to remain at the ranch when others, like themselves, had gone through comparable tests and had 'flown the coop'? The answer was simple. Robert stayed because of the strong conviction he had gained during the marvelous experience that had taken place within him some years before.

Ten years later, the Casper family moved away from the ranch. They had experienced countless, severe trials and tribulations. Robert had taught Concept Therapy for fifteen years and he knew that the time was fast approaching when the vision he had beheld would start to manifest. He knew that all he had gone through had been for the purpose of preparing him to be able to manifest the vision on the physical plane.

THE VISION

During his marvelous experience in 1960, Robert beheld a vision that might be described as a waking dream. During the vision, Robert saw three separate scenes. Each scene depicted a different phase of the development of Eo-Wa-Ta, the place in Robert's vision. Robert later referred to these phases as the development phase, the establishment phase and the completion phase.

In the development phase of the vision, he saw a beautiful place where children were listening to a young instructor presenting a lesson. Upon completion of the lesson, the instructor dismissed the children and informed them that they were free to go and play. In the dream, Robert approached the instructor and asked him, "What is this place? What is its purpose?" The instructor informed him that it was a summer camp for children known as Camp Eo-Wa-Ta. He offered to take Robert on a tour, and Robert accepted. As they walked along, he told Robert about the Camp and also showed him pictures of what was to be built in the future.

They left the covered pavilion where the class had been held and headed for a bright yellow, single-story structure which he called the administration building. They then passed by four large, single-story buildings, also bright yellow in color, and arrived at the end of a large, wooded area. From this location, they could observe open, rolling hills that he said someday would also be part of Camp Eo-Wa-Ta. Then they retraced their steps past the administration building, through a gate, and onto a gravel road.

Turning to their right, they walked down the gravel road past more rolling hills to their left and a wooded area to their right. The instructor told Robert that the wooded area to the right was already part of the Camp and that the hills to the left would also be part of Eo-Wa-Ta someday. The instructor noticed a quizzical look on Robert's face, and so he said to him, "You are wondering what the name Eo-Wa-Ta means. Robert, the meaning of the name will be revealed to you at a later time." He went on to say that Camp Eo-Wa-Ta would consist of three sections, each with its own director: the *Eo*, the *Wa* and the *Ta*. The first of these sections was the children's camp, the place they had just visited. He referred to this area as the *Ta* section.

Next, they approached the main entrance of Camp Eo-Wa-Ta. At the entrance were two large stone columns supporting two metal gates. As they passed between the columns, the young instructor informed Robert that when the three Camp directors could function as one expression, a huge lighted rainbow would be erected that would span from one column to the other. Inside the gates, there were beautiful shrubs and bushes bordering the gravel road on both sides. Robert immediately became conscious of nine lilac bushes; lilacs had always been his favorite flowers. All the flowers and plants on the left of the road were blue, while on the opposite side, they were different shades of yellow. Just ahead to the left was a beautiful flowered area. Within it was a large fountain in the shape of a pyramid. To the right was a huge, bright yellow building. The instructor said, "We are now in the *Wa* section of the Camp. This large building is the mess hall." Again, the instructor noticed Robert's quizzical look and said, "The *Wa* section of the Camp is the teaching center. People from all over the world come here for instruction based on a new philosophy of life."

Ahead of them was a large, circular area with several paths through it. In front of them and along the paths were more beautiful flowerbeds. The particular path they followed led to a large, brick patio. Within and around the patio were more flowerbeds and in the center was a large, blue spruce tree. The entire area surrounding the patio was a huge circle. South from the patio was another path leading back to the gravel road that surrounded the entire area. Where the path ended, the gravel road continued southward. The instructor said, "The area down this road is the *Eo* section of the Camp, where you and others will have homes. At this time, we will not go any further." With those words, the vision ended, just as if a curtain had closed upon the first act of a play.

After this, Robert began to reflect on the statements he had heard throughout the tour. He had been given the assignment of fulfilling this vision and finding dedicated individuals who would help build Eo-Wa-Ta. In addition, he was told that he would behold two more visions so that he could see the plan in its entirety.

During the tour, the instructor had made many predictions about the consciousness of man. "Soon a great destroying force will come that will especially affect children. Camp Eo-Wa-Ta will be a counter force that will teach children a new, constructive philosophy of life, showing them the wonders of creation. A period is beginning to manifest when law and order will break down. Crime and vice will take over the consciousness of our youth, and unless a new, scientific knowledge of life is made available, this destructive force will destroy civilization. The present religious and educational systems will not be able to cope with the problem. Young people will try to escape by resorting to drugs and the practice of pseudo-science or the occult. Others will attempt to escape with fanatical religious zeal. However, a new philosophy of the *one life* will come into the consciousness of man through the findings of science, the music of composers, the lyrics of songwriters, and the words of authors. This new philosophy will not destroy any of the teachings of the great spiritual founders, but instead will reveal the true meaning of these teachings from a scientific viewpoint. Camp Eo-Wa-Ta will be the place where all can observe the expansion of consciousness." Robert recalled asking the instructor where this Camp would be built. The instructor told him that, "It will be built in the land of the great Sioux Nation, between two mighty rivers."

As Robert continued to dwell upon these words, he began to experience another scene. Robert was a passenger in a small two-seater airplane. It was a beautiful, clear, sunny day, and below him he could observe all the details of the landscape, the rolling farmlands and the wooded areas. Suddenly he realized that the paved road that he was observing was the same gravel road he had previously walked along with the instructor. The plane was gradually descending, coming to a landing in an area being worked on with heavy equipment. It appeared as if a large parking area was being constructed.

Before he could observe all the grounds, the plane had landed and was taxiing towards a small hangar. After the plane came to a stop, Robert opened the door of the plane, stepped out, and once again saw the smiling instructor. He welcomed Robert to Camp Eo-Wa-Ta a second time and said, "It's been a long time since you were last here. Camp Eo-Wa-Ta is reaching the final stage of its establishment phase. Come, I will take you on another tour."

As they drove toward the paved road, he pointed out some other construction that was in progress. He said, "That building now going up will be the motel and restaurant for patients, and the site next to it will be the location of our health clinic."

They first returned to the *Ta* section, the children's camp. As they turned right onto the paved road, Robert observed, on his left, small buildings and cages containing animals. The instructor informed him that this was the zoo that they would visit on their way back. They next observed other buildings and beautiful displays of plants. The instructor informed Robert that this area was the botanical garden. Ahead of them, they could once again see the administration building, and standing next to it, two pavilions and a newly erected flagpole. Before they arrived at the administration building, they passed a rock-covered, barren area that the instructor said represented the inanimate phase of life. Then they passed by a row of cedar trees towards a large wooden gateway. Above the gates was a lattice spanning two columns with the letters *EO-WA-TA*. The gateway and the letters were all made of wooden logs.

Straight ahead of them was the road leading to the far side of the Camp. Instead of going down this road, they turned left and went down the curved, stone-covered road leading to the administration building. On both sides of this road were flowerbeds and in front of the building were other plants and shrubs. They walked into the office of the administration building and were greeted by a young woman, "Welcome to the *Ta* section of Camp Eo-Wa-Ta."

She explained that the staff was preparing for the following weeks' children's camp and that they were expecting nearly one hundred children to attend. After looking around the office, they returned to the road leading to the far side of the Camp. As they walked down this road, they saw, on their right, an area for recreational sports, and on their left, a building with restrooms and showers. Further down the road, they passed by four barrack buildings, two on each side of the road, which were sleeping quarters for the children. Far to their left, they observed a pond that was to hold wastewater.

Robert also noticed the foliage that was just as beautiful as he had remembered it to be during his last visit. At the far end of the Camp there was a large, cylindrically shaped building with a dome top. "This," said the instructor, "is our observatory. Nightly, programs are held here that are open to the public." Inside the observatory there were seats positioned around the room facing a screen. The remaining walls were completely covered with paintings of stars and galaxies. The instructor informed him that the audience could view on the screen what was actually being sighted with the telescope, situated above them in the dome.

They next went outside and climbed an iron stairway to the dome itself. Inside the dome was a large refracting telescope and a stand holding electronic equipment. Robert was amazed at all he had seen, but was told that this was just the beginning of what he was to see before leaving. The instructor told Robert that the purpose of the observatory was to show the one life principle ruling the entire cosmos. By observing the heavens, a student could become conscious of the power, the majesty and the glory of the infinite creative essence.

Downstairs in the observatory, Robert witnessed the first act of the play "Life". The entire audience was experiencing the beginning of creation and the formation of the heavens. On the ceiling was a scale model of the solar system. As they left the observatory, they saw a large, orange, domed structure representing a star. The instructor informed Robert that inside this building, one could witness the birth, the life and the death of stars.

They then got into a Jeep and drove up to the inanimate phase, finally coming to a stop in front of a volcano. Robert was informed that this was where the second act of the play "Life" took place. As his guide took him to the entrance of a cave, Robert observed a large model of the planet Earth. The instructor told Robert that they were going to take a journey to the center of the Earth.

After their journey through the caves, they left the inanimate phase and proceeded to a smaller, green, domed structure. The instructor told Robert that this was the single-cell building and it represented the beginning of the animate phase of the play, "Life".

Next, they went into another building and observed fish and other aquatic animals. At this point, the instructor informed Robert that they would be observing the different classes of animate forms. The exhibit showed the development from the single cells to the amphibians, then the reptiles, the birds, the marsupials and finally the mammals. This whole area was filled with beautiful plants and flowers.

After completing their tour of the zoo, they left the animate phase and walked over to a dock on a small river. There, waiting for them, was a scaled replica of Robert Fulton's first steamboat, the Clermont. They boarded the boat and traveled the river back to the *Wa* section of Eo-Wa-Ta.

By that time it was growing dark, and Robert knew it was time for him to leave. As they drove back to the airstrip to say good-bye, Robert asked if there had been any other changes made in other areas of the Camp. He asked especially about the rainbow, and if it had yet been built over the entrance gate. His guide pointed and directed Robert's attention towards the gates. There, Robert saw the diffused light of many colors glowing in the darkness. Again, as though a curtain descended, the second act of the vision faded away.

After this, Robert was in a state of bewilderment. Before the third and final part of the vision, Robert again had time to reflect on what he had seen. He slowly came to the realization that this beautiful experience had revealed to him the principles of creation and facts concerning the origin of the universe. He knew then that he had actually been in tune with the consciousness of the one life.

After this realization, he began to experience another vision. This time, he was again at Eo-Wa-Ta and was leaving the dining room of the mess hall. To the left, a short distance away, Robert saw a large wooden building with a long line of people waiting to enter it. He recognized that the place where the building stood used to be a parking lot.

Feeling a tug at his arm, Robert turned around and once again saw his friend, the instructor. He told Robert that Camp Eo-Wa-Ta was complete. It had been completed when Fleet's Hall, the final building on the Camp, was erected and opened to the public. He said that the people lined up in front of the hall had just completed the afternoon tour of creation at the children's camp. He referred to this tour as the play, "Life". He went on to say that, "These people will go into the building and enter into an environment where they can experience the evolution of consciousness. They will be able to become conscious of the infinite creative essence expressing in all life. Finally, the group will listen to an informative presentation of the one life philosophy before they leave the building."

After leaving Fleet's Hall, Robert and his guide once again toured the entire Camp. Robert asked the instructor how many people were living at Camp Eo-Wa-Ta at that time. The guide told Robert that there were thirty-six families and that the members of these families constituted the entire staff. All of the members worked under the direction of the three camp directors who were then working together as one entity known as *EOWATA*.

Robert asked his guide how and when Camp Eo-Wa-Ta would be built on the physical plane. He was still wondering whether all he had seen was just a dream. The instructor replied, "No, this is not a dream. Eo-Wa-Ta will be built by you and by those who will be guided here."

Robert again asked, "Where is this place and how can I locate it?" The instructor replied with words that Robert would never forget. "You will build this camp in the land of the Sioux, between the two mighty rivers. It is a place where young and old can behold the wonders of creation. You will be guided by signs and will receive help from invisible sources when the time comes."

When the instructor finished speaking, the vision faded from Robert's view. It did not, however, fade from Robert's memory. The vision left such a vivid impression on Robert that he could re-experience it at any time. He knew that the vision was real, and it never dimmed in his consciousness. Robert knew that some day, in some way, he would be directed at the appointed time to manifest the vision on the physical plane. For Robert, Eo-Wa-Ta was the most beautiful place on Earth. There, he could feel the presence of the infinite power radiating its divine love and spirit through every rock, blade of grass, flower, leaf, tree, animal and human being.

THE MANIFESTATION OF THE VISION

Near a small town in southwestern Iowa, on an eighty-eight acre tract of timberland, the vision Robert had seen so long before was manifesting. Reflecting back to that ten-day experience, it seemed to Robert that he had been assigned an almost impossible task. However, there he was, standing upon an eighty-foot patio, looking out towards the mess hall and towards Rainbow Drive, leading through the main entrance of Camp Eo-Wa-Ta.

Almost forty years had come and gone since Robert's experience. On many occasions, Robert recalled how he had first embarked upon the journey to find his destiny and the influence that Dr. Fleet's teaching had on him. He recalled how he had left his employment and his home and moved to Texas to study under Dr. Thurman Fleet. Robert prized the knowledge he gained from Fleet's teachings above all else and he had a tremendous respect for him. He knew that Dr. Fleet had devoted his life to organizing and teaching a philosophy of the one life. The sole purpose of the Concept Therapy philosophy was to raise the consciousness of its members from that of separated self-consciousness to the consciousness of the one life. Fleet referred to this higher consciousness as *fourth dimensional consciousness*. Dr. Fleet had devoted forty years of his life to elevating his students to a position where they could make the decision to renounce their personal selves, their third dimensional consciousness. He knew that only then could they accept and truly live the one life philosophy.

Prior to having been introduced to Concept Therapy, Robert had spent nearly all his life searching for the answers to his questions. All his findings had intellectually convinced him that there was only one Creative Essence, or God, expressing through everything that existed. There was nothing else. However, it was not until he had thoroughly applied Dr. Fleet's teachings that he had his vision and thereby came to *experience* the oneness of life.

After his experience in 1960, Robert taught Concept Therapy classes with only one objective in mind. He wanted to get his students to think on their own in order that they too would someday arrive at the same conclusions he had and have a similar experience. During his many years of teaching, the vision Robert beheld never faded from his consciousness. Robert always remembered how, during his vision, he had been promised help in building Eo-Wa-Ta. Everywhere Robert went, he looked for dedicated individuals who would want to assist in bringing the vision into manifestation. Robert did not know how long it would take to manifest the vision nor where he would find those individuals, but he never wavered from the task of looking for help.

After teaching over two hundred classes, Robert finally found a few unselfish individuals who could accept the one life aspect and who could dedicate their time and effort to help build Eo-Wa-Ta. Camp Eo-Wa-Ta could not be built to serve personal needs. It had to be built to manifest the power, the glory and the majesty of the one infinite Creative Essence.

By 1970, it became evident that he had found the nucleus of individuals he had been looking for. After teaching a class in Kansas City, Missouri, Robert and several members of this new group were driving to South Bend, Indiana. While driving there, Robert was inclined to ask those in the car to look at a map of the State of Iowa. He asked them to note any town that had the letter X contained in its name. Robert told them that this town would also have to be near the intersection of two highways whose digits totaled a multiple of eight. Looking at the map, they found a town named Exira near the intersection of Interstate 80 and US 71. They decided to take a detour and visit the small town.

After arriving in Exira, Robert became conscious that within a thirty-mile radius they would find the site upon which they would build Camp Eo-Wa-Ta. They located the real estate office owned by a Mr. Young. After Robert described the details of the land he had seen in his vision, Mr. Young informed the group that he thought he had the place they were looking for. On the way out to the property with Mr. Young, they drove through the town of Anita. Robert thought it was quite a coincidence because *Anita* was the name of a member of the group.

The group, guided by the realtor, eventually arrived at a gravel road that led straight to the property. They spent most of the afternoon inspecting and walking around as much of the property as they could. By the time they left the acreage, Robert knew that it was the place he was looking for; this was the future location of Eo-Wa-Ta. Although the property was overgrown with trees, brush and weeds, Robert was certain that this was the place he had seen in his vision.

Robert knew that the image of Eo-Wa-Ta was beginning to attract other individuals to the property. There were so many coincidences during the initial few years that it would be difficult for anyone to believe. These experiences, however, convinced Robert that his vision had been real and not simply a normal dream. It amazed Robert how a place like Eo-Wa-Ta, with only woods and insects to offer, attracted two professional artists and many others to come, live and be a vital part of an unseen plan. Over the following years, many people came to live at Eo-Wa-Ta and to help in its development.

It came as no surprise that the residents of Bridgewater, and other nearby communities, could not comprehend what was taking place. Many of the local citizens spread rumors as to why strangers from all over came to live in the woods of Iowa. But how could they have known what was happening? Very few of them ever came out to investigate and see for themselves what was taking place. To some, the group was building a nudist camp, to others, they were a communist group planning secret warfare, and yet to others, they were building a hippie commune.

Despite the rumors that were circulating, the group at Eo-Wa-Ta went to work – and my did they *work*! By the time the second year's birthday celebration rolled around, they had cleared a large area of trees and had constructed the mess hall and an eighty-foot diameter patio. Each successive year, they cleared more and more ground, and as donations came in, they continued to make improvements and construct more buildings. For the next twenty-five years, the group worked steadily in building and improving the Camp. Each year brought a greater consciousness to those who lived at and helped build Eo-Wa-Ta.

Because of the slow development and limited funds available to the group, many of the members became discouraged and left. Other individuals eventually came to replace them. Robert knew that the seed had been planted. The vision of Eo-Wa-Ta that had been given to him was beginning to manifest. Eo-Wa-Ta's development was like a seed bursting forth its first shoots. The seed would face storms, extremes of temperature and many unforeseen obstacles. Robert also knew, however, that the seed had the ability to adapt and would eventually develop and reveal the image that was locked up within it. The development of Eo-Wa-Ta had begun and some day, in some way, it would fully manifest in all its glory.

One evening, while walking on the patio, Robert reflected on Eo-Wa-Ta's development and marveled at the peace he felt there. Then he thought about how man had worshiped, sacrificed and even faced martyrdom in order to be rewarded when he died. Many continue to believe today that this afterlife, which man calls heaven, is his reward for living a good life, and can only be experienced after death. He believes that heaven is a physical place that he goes to when he dies. However, when the Pharisees demanded to know when the kingdom of God would come, Jesus replied, "Neither shall they say, Lo here! or, Lo there! for, behold, the kingdom of God is within you".

Robert knew that this saying of Jesus was true and he also knew that when the vision of Eo-Wa-Ta was manifested in its entirety, one would find a little bit of that heaven in the southwest corner of the state of Iowa.

THE ASSIGNMENT

During his marvelous vision, Robert was given an assignment consisting of three parts: manifesting Eo-Wa-Ta on the physical plane, writing a book and teaching the philosophy of the one life. After he received it, he knew that he would willingly spend the rest of his life completing the assignment.

Almost forty years had passed since Robert beheld the vision in which he received his assignment. The first part of the assignment had nearly been completed. Camp Eo-Wa-Ta was steadily progressing towards completion. Robert knew that in another few years, the manifestation of Eo-Wa-Ta on the physical plane would fully reflect the vision he had witnessed in 1960.

Twenty years prior, Robert had spent time writing and recording passages that eventually were compiled into a book. This was the second part of the assignment he had been given. Robert had been told that someday he would write a book that described how one had found his path to truth. When the manuscript was completed, the group combined their efforts and gave financial support to have the book published and distributed.

For twenty years after his experience, and for ten years at Eo-Wa-Ta, Robert continued to teach Concept Therapy to his students. Finally, in 1979, Robert came to the realization that it was necessary to teach the one life philosophy from a rational, scientific perspective. He separated himself completely from the Concept Therapy Institute and began to teach a new course of instruction. Soon after, the group applied for and received federal government recognition as a tax exempt, non-profit, scientific, educational organization. For the rest of Robert's life, he lived at Eo-Wa-Ta and taught this new philosophy throughout the United States and Canada. This was the third and final part of the assignment, and until the day he died, Robert never wavered from trying to raise the consciousness of those around him through this teaching.

For many years, Robert's students asked him to try to explain what transpired during his 1960 experience. On many occasions, he informally described what he had witnessed and tried to explain its significance. In February 1999, Robert wrote down some notes, explaining in detail the entire ten-day experience. The following passage is a transcription of those notes.

"Many of you have asked me to explain the experience of 1960. It will be difficult to explain but I shall endeavor to do so. Most of you, or I should say all of you, have had dreams, and some of these dreams have later become manifest on the physical plane. All through my life, as far as I can recall, I have had occasions where dreams have come to me that later manifested in the external world.

In trying to comprehend how these dreams came to pass, and after having done much research, I could only conclude, as a theory, that those dreams that later manifested must have existed on another plane of consciousness. Daily, all of us see the world around us through our external senses but at night, when we retire, we lose all consciousness of the physical plane. From this we would have to conclude that when we dream, these dreams come to us from our own inner world.

When we dream, the dreams are usually associated with abnormal vibrations of brain cell activity, the activation of previous awareness. This activates other associated awareness, and we dream of past, antecedent conditions. Occasionally, we have a dream that is not entirely based on antecedent experiences but is in tune with some other space-time dimension, revealing to us things that are to occur on the physical plane at a later time. We would have to conclude that if we had a dream that later manifested on the physical plane, then in some way, we were in another space-time dimension.

This is one way that I can explain to you how you might dream of things yet to come. Can you imagine a time when you would not only dream at night but would also dream during the day, when you were wide-awake and fully conscious of the external plane? In 1960, I had an experience in which I was not only more conscious of the external world but, at the same time, I was also more in touch with the other realm, another space-time dimension. Image, if you will, that you could become conscious of the physical world and then, at will, blot it out and become fully conscious of the inner world.

You know, when we speak of our consciousness, even of the external, we admit that these vibrations add energy to awareness, making us conscious. We should also recognize that we are separated from our inner world when the energy of our environment is greater than the energy coming from our inner world. At night, when you retire and go to sleep, you lose all consciousness of the external plane. You might say that when you dream, you are conscious of the inner plane within you. In other words, we might say that the threshold of consciousness, or the psychic barrier, is

145

removed or partially removed. When you are fully awake, that barrier is once again closed and you only become conscious of your environment.

Can you imagine if your psychic barrier had been fully opened and that you could open and close it at will? You might think of it as a door, or a gate, which you had the ability to open and close at will. In 1960, for some unknown reason, this took place in my life. During the day, I was fully conscious of the external world but all I had to do was to hold my thought on the inner plane and I would be able to blot out the external realm and be conscious of the inner world.

Imagine, during this time, that you were able to blot out the physical world and automatically become conscious of this dream-like inner world. There were people, there were events, there were scenes and there was communication. You would think that your dream was real, but when you woke up in the morning, you either retained some part of the dream, you were fully conscious of the dream or you lost all memory of it. Now imagine that you could lie in bed at night, being fully awake and fully conscious of the external world – the bed, the room, and the furniture in the room – and at the same time enter into this dream world.

It may, at first, appear to be a frightening experience, but then you discover there is no fear while in this state. This is because of your knowledge of the teaching of the inner plane that you have received in the past. You have no fear of what is happening. If you did not have the knowledge of how the human personality works and the knowledge of the physical, mental and spiritual planes of existence, it would be logical that you might imagine yourself developing a dual or schizophrenic personality.

You are now conscious that this inner plane exists, but one can only be conscious of it from abnormal brain cell functions, abnormal activation of awareness. Imagine that you could come home, sit outside alone and automatically contact this other plane or space-time dimension. It is just as real as this world you live in and observe with your senses. Trying to comprehend this, you would have to conclude that you had gained some inner senses that enable you to see, hear, touch, taste and smell things on this other plane. This plane would be just as real as the physical plane.

For a period of ten days, I found myself being able to be in these two planes of existence at the same time. At first, it was rather confusing, for it seemed as if one plane was superimposed upon the other. After a short period, it seemed like I could turn off one plane and then enter the other. It was very amusing to talk to someone in my office, and after having them leave, to talk to others on another plane. If anyone had come into the office during that time, they would, perhaps, have thought the individual sitting there was a little bit out of his mind. But usually, I would refrain from communicating with this other plane until I was alone.

While this was going on, I found that I had a great desire to communicate with this other world and I found that I wanted to be left alone. For these ten days, I spent most evenings communicating with this other world. There were actual beings, or personalities, just as there are on this plane. Now, that does not mean to say that I could see them with my physical eyes. No. I do not want to give you the idea that these individuals appeared physically. They only appear within you. So, we might call this an inner world.

In other words, the soul who is capable of existing on the external plane is also capable of entering this other plane of awareness. While in this other plane, I was told many things and saw many events. At first, I did not know whether these events would ever materialize on the physical plane or not. But, there seemed to be an assurance in talking with these people in that they were truthful and that they would tell me what was going to happen. I call them entities. During this time, I became conscious of many things that would happen to me on the physical plane in, what we might call, a future space-time.

I am not going into the details concerning my experiences with the Institute: going to work, going back into industry, then coming back into the Concept Therapy Institute and all of that. But all of this was shown to me during my experience. At one point, I saw Camp Eo-Wa-Ta. I saw it in all its detail and all its beauty, and nothing that I can think of will ever stop it from manifesting. But again, we do not know, just as in a dream, when an event is going to occur. Like watching a movie, a whole lifetime goes by on the screen in a relatively short period of time.

So there is no way of telling the time or the year in this other dimension. For in this other dimension, it already exists. But there is no way of knowing when it is going to manifest on the physical plane. All I can say is, after the experience, I was more or less in a quandary, wondering if these things I had seen and heard would really materialize.

During this experience, I was taught about the Bhagavad Gita and the Bible, and we would hold discussions concerning parts of these books. Then, the next day, when I was able to shut off this inner plane, I would then take the Bhagavad Gita and the Bible and look up some of the things we spoke about while I was in contact with this other plane of existence. I was amazed to find the exact references in these texts in which they had instructed me.

I took the Bhagavad Gita and underlined the major topics in which I was instructed, and now I want to show you the passages that I underlined. You may want to purchase the Bhagavad Gita, by Yogi Ramacharaka, from The Yogi Publication Society, Copyright 1930 (ISBN #0-911662-10-3). The following are some of the passages I underlined. The first was from the Chapter, 'The Inner Doctrine', page thirty-five: 'Free thyself from the pair of opposites – the changeful things of finite life'. Next, from page thirty-eight: 'Such a man meets the charges and events of life, be they favorable or unfavorable, with equanimity – likes and dislikes being foreign to him'. Next, from page thirty-nine: 'Wrapt in contemplation of the Real, the unreal exists not for him.' From the Chapter, 'The Secret of Work', page fifty-one: 'The senses are great and powerful; but greater and more powerful than the Senses is the Mind; and greater than the Mind is the Will; and greater than the Will is the Real Self.'

This little book gave me the greatest insights into what I was experiencing. The main purpose of our instruction can be summarized by this passage in the Chapter, 'Spiritual Discernment' on page eighty-five: 'But those who are wise and are able to know Me as Myself – the All – the One – such come to Me in My world of Reality'.

After conversing in these two worlds for ten days, this other world became more real than the external plane in which we live. It seemed to me as if the external plane was an extension of the inner plane; it was the part of that plane that was manifesting at the time. When I was in contact with this inner world, I was also conscious of what I was doing on the external world at that time.

In these experiences in the inner world, there was no effort or work employed. And even though I was still in the external world during this period, I was conscious that everything I was doing was effortless. In other words, the external world was there, but it was of a different density. It was almost as if the trees and the leaves were transparent, that people were of a transparent nature. And for periods of time, it seemed as if I could be inside the people themselves. I was able to know their feelings, their pains, and their aches. It seemed as if they were part of me, and yet, I was not entirely a part of them.

Then for periods of time during this experience, both worlds would completely disappear, and it seemed as if there was a feeling of warmth while a rose colored hue took over my vision. And during that period, there was a feeling of love and closeness that was indescribable. Maybe you could get the idea, provided you liked rose or orchid colors, of feeling yourself enter a room where everything was colored. The colors were completely unimaginable.

Perhaps some of you saw the motion picture '2001: A Space Odyssey'. Recall when the man's consciousness went through all those colors. Then there was a scene where the colors were vivid and bright: white, pinkish and purple. Well, it seemed as if this external world appeared that way during that period. It was almost transparent and yet I was able to feel and know exactly what was going on within the personalities I came in contact with. Now this is hard to describe, I know, but I am trying as simply as I can to explain something that I just cannot find adequate words for.

But while in this state and this time-space continuum, I actually found myself at Camp Eo-Wa-Ta. And I saw this camp in the most beautiful setting that you could possibly conceive of. And since it has been manifesting on the physical plane, I am more and more convinced that someday this camp and this area will manifest in its entirety in accordance with that which I perceived in 1960.

Now, we realize that consciousness will be affected by the programs of those living on the physical plane, in just the same way as if I should take an image of a home to an architect. The architect has his own ideas as to how things should be done, and unless one was able to see that the architect interjected some of his own views, then the finished plans would be somewhat distorted. So, in order to manifest this dream in its entirety, I was given an assignment. My mission, as Eo-Wa-Ta began to develop, was to make sure that, even though there would be temporary modifications to the plans due to circumstances on the physical plane, the end result of the manifestation would be the same as the original image. The plans would have to be continually revised and updated until eventually, someday in the future, the manifestation would be an exact duplicate of the image in all its detail.

Now, the roads coming into the camp, some of the buildings and the layouts are not the complete picture of what will be. That's ridiculous. But the image is in existence and is manifesting. And as time goes by, refinements will be made to existing manifestations. And just like your consciousness is in a state of evolution, the overall consciousness of the camp will continue to evolve, year by year, until it has reached its full, complete manifestation. What the consciousness is to be already exists in this other realm.

I can also tell you that during this time it was difficult to be normal like others who are strictly conscious of the outer world. I had the consciousness, when dealing with the external world, that I was frightening people by some of my actions. Things were happening on the external world that appeared to be phenomena. Some of my friends, who came into my presence at the time, were literally amazed how predictions were made and how events that had already happened to them were expressed through this form. And so, this form became conscious that it was frightening others, and after ten days, it begged the power to remove the consciousness, or again, to set up the wall so that there was no way the door would be open between these two worlds.

We explained that this psychic barrier is the wall that separates one from the spirit within. You can imagine what would happen if this barrier was removed. We are teaching our students that the barrier can be removed, and that you can enter into this other world. Now, one might ask, 'Is this world the etheric plane or is this world the astral plane?' Our only answer is that on the astral plane, just as it is on the physical plane, there exists the pair of opposites. There are the pros and the cons, the light and the dark, the good and the bad. But, when one enters this other plane there are no opposites. All is beauty and all is truth, and everything that is said must be lowered into an interpretation within you before it is manifested on the physical plane.

One would have to assume that since these pictures or these images were not already impressed upon my brain cells or the mental plane, then they must have come from a plane that is not of the mental realm. In order for one to communicate on the mental plane, as we know, there must be similar awareness between the sender and the receiver. Since

I knew none of this material and had never had these experiences on the mental plane, I would have to assume that there was a plane superior, primary and causative to the other two planes.

After the experiences were over, I could then meditate or concentrate upon what had taken place. At that time, I was using the mental plane. But during the time when the communication was being presented and when the scenes were unfolding, it seemed as if these images and scenes were placed from this other plane into this form's awareness. These images and scenes had never previously existed in my consciousness. It was as if these images were impressed as suggestions in my subconscious, much like when an operator impresses ideas into the awareness of a hypnotized subject. It seemed as if this other plane of existence, these other entities, were operators that were capable of placing their images and their ideas into the subconscious fabric of this form. In other words, we might say, these were post-hypnotic suggestions that have influenced, guided and inclined me, on the physical plane, to let nothing stand in the way of having the images manifest. It was as if I was hypnotized to a great idea and accepted it as a divine mission.

I do not know any other way to explain to you how this comes about. There is a causative plane that, we might say, is superimposed upon the physical and the mental planes of existence. This plane can reach down to someone that is on the mental plane who can then receive from this etheric plane, just in the same way as you carry out your thoughts on the physical plane. So, imagine if you could reach the point where the physical plane, or we call it the carnal plane, the external world, has become less enslaving to you. Then you, possibly, would, in consciousness, give up this external world. Then, the only other plane you could live on would be the mental plane. And then, just as your thought world influences your physical plane, you will then be able to receive, from time to time, images that come to your mental realm from the etheric plane. Until finally, the time may come when you will be able to consciously live on the etheric plane, or if you want, call it the highest plane. Then you are in touch with the causative plane of existence and you will then know, beyond a shadow of a doubt, that these guiding forces from this plane of existence are the creative principles of the entire universe.

At first, images from the etheric plane are impressed on the astral plane as awareness in the form. Then, the awareness on the astral plane, the middle plane, gets mixed up by some images coming from the higher plane and some information coming from the physical plane. Then you can see that the astral plane would have periods of what we might call hell and periods of heaven. So, we say the astral plane is a state of awareness of a hellish nature, the lower astral plane, or of a heavenly nature, the higher astral plane. But beyond both is this causative plane where there is nothing but the eternal.

To describe this plane of existence, one would have to realize that every time they have a dream on the astral plane that eventually manifests on the physical plane, that dream must have come from the higher etheric realm. Knowing this, there is no longer any doubt that there is an infinite intelligence guiding, directing, and ruling the entire universe. It does this by projecting itself into the inner consciousness of the forms. But, the forms being mixed up because of their external senses, become conscious of the external world, and therefore, these two worlds collide in the mental plane.

Now, as one practices, he will free himself from the consciousness of the physical plane. That does not mean giving up anything. That does not mean selling everything. It means looking at the physical plane the way you now look at the dream world, as if the physical plane is a dream. And as your consciousness continues to expand, you will live in your physical realm the same way you live when you are in your dream world. Eventually, you will find yourself thinking of the external world, when you wake up, as the dream world that you just entered, and the dream world will be the world that you really live in, the world you just left. As you exclude the physical, external environment – the people, the places and the things around you – then you will become a receptacle for the higher world to be in resonance with your awareness, making you conscious of the images and ideas that exist on the etheric plane.

I am not asking you to believe this, to accept it or to reject it. I am just trying to convey to you that, unless I'm nuts, Camp Eo-Wa-Ta already exists and someday it must manifest as a duplication of the image that now exists in the etheric. We will go on building Eo-Wa-Ta to the best of our ability and with the funds and resources we receive. We will slowly and surely refine our image of building Eo-Wa-Ta, until someday, our image is at one with the etheric image of Eo-Wa-Ta, and the Camp will be manifested here on the physical plane in all its perfection. I believe that this is described in the Lord's prayer: 'Thy kingdom come. Thy will be done, as in heaven, so in earth.'

I hope that this will give you some idea of the state of consciousness that each one of you, even now, are in contact with, but have blinded yourself from. You are blinded by seeing with your physical eyes, hearing with your physical ears, tasting, touching and smelling with your physical senses. But, as you begin to apply what we have taught you and you begin to understand it, your consciousness will rise above the physical. You will become free of the physical and live, at least, on the mental or astral realm. Close the door to the carnal plane and live in the mental realm, gradually improving this mental realm so that you become more receptive to the etheric. Just as some people improve their state of awareness so that they can dream more clearly and more often, so too will you receive dreams originating from the etheric plane. So you might say, 'As above, so below'. Just like you dream on the mental realm while your physical body is sleeping, so too will the etheric plane become a dream in your mental body. When that happens, you will know that you are in touch with the primary source of life itself. You will become conscious of the oneness of it all, and no longer will you have any doubt that you live, have always lived and will never die. You only die to the first and second planes of existence: the physical and the mental. You will understand that he who escapes the 'second death' will live in the eternal, meaning that, right now, your mental plane is keeping you separated from the highest realm.

So, our first step is to free ourselves of the carnal plane so that we can live in the mental realm. Know the mental realm. Change the mental realm. Clean up the old associations that you have with the physical realm. This Camp, we might say, is an etheric dream that was lowered down onto the mental realm, as its physical manifestation was planned. Now, that dream is coming into existence on the physical plane. Can you image how beautiful Eo-Wa-Ta will be when the dream has been perfected on the physical plane? I can."

The Greatest Mystery

Throughout this book, Robert Casper has been depicted as an individual who forged a path and set out on a mission to find the reason for his existence and to find answers to his own questions: who am I, why am I here, and what is my goal and destiny?

In the past, there were individuals who, at some time in their lives, had a mystical experience and, after the experience, began to teach their fellowman how he should live. They taught how man should conduct himself in order to gain freedom from enslavement and a more abundant life. Upon the death of these great teachers, those followers who did not understand the higher meaning of their teachings, elevated these teachers to a status of a god. They proclaimed that the teachers had performed supernatural feats: healing the incurable, changing water into wine, walking on water, parting the seas, etc. These teachers were attributed with overcoming natural law, even to the point of bringing the dead back to life.

By elevating them in this manner, their followers enslaved themselves to the great teachers. In similar manner, these followers, with their limited understanding, enslaved others into also believing that the great teachers were more than human. This was truly the 'blind leading the blind'. Thereafter, the followers formed organized religions and allowed themselves to be subjected to the authority of the priests and heads of the churches. This authoritative power gave the church leaders control over nations and control over the life and death of each follower. This physical, mental and spiritual enslavement was the greatest tragedy *ever* to befall mankind. This enslavement was in direct opposition to what had been taught by the great teachers. According to the Scriptures, they taught the way to freedom and peace and how to love one another.

Moses, the founder of the Hebrew religion, freed his people from slavery and led them to the gates of the Promised Land. Buddha taught the eight-fold path in order to free his fellow man from suffering. Jesus said, "I am come that they might have life, and that they might have it more abundantly." Another time, Jesus said, "All these things I do, ye can do", and, "Know the truth and the truth will make you free". All of these teachings must have been forgotten by the masses. Those who became the religious authorities took it upon themselves to condemn anyone whose findings or conclusions disagreed with church dogma.

Down through the ages, many marveled at the beauty and glory of creation but accepted, on faith alone, that a divine being created it all. These individuals felt that man should not investigate nor seek to know how or why a divine being created it all. They were taught by their religions that scientific investigation into the nature of the divine being was sacrilegious.

Fortunately, throughout history, there have always been philosophers who had a love for wisdom and wanted to know. These men were not content to merely view creation with awe and acceptance. They wanted to investigate it in order to know the nature of all things. As they continually sought, studied and experimented, the knowledge they gained became so vast that there soon became a need for specialized, specific fields of investigation. These specific fields of study developed into what we now call the *sciences*. As the scientists gained more knowledge, the facts concerning creation became a threat to the established religious systems.

Perhaps the greatest threat to the religions was the theory of evolution. Somehow, in their limited view, the creationists believed that evolution denied the very existence of God. To Christians, it denied the account of creation described in *the Book of Genesis*. One who really wishes to know the truth must investigate this account. Robert found that the sequence of events during creation in the *Genesis* account did not differ from the findings of science. The two accounts of creation appear to contradict each other *only* in the length of time it took for creation to take place.

Genesis states that, on the first day, there was light. "God said, Let there be light; and there was light." Science states that at the moment of the Big Bang, light appeared and filled the universe. *Genesis* states that on the second day, "And God said, Let there be a firmament in the midst of the waters, and let it divide the waters from the waters." Science states that the second step of creation was the formation of hydrogen, the basic element of water. Science also knows that this hydrogen produced the stars and galaxies that span the entire cosmos.

Genesis describes the formation of the Earth during the third day of creation.

> *And God said, Let the waters under the heavens be gathered together unto one place, and let the dry land appear; and it was so. And God called the dry land Earth; and the gathering together of the waters called He seas: and God saw that it was good. And God said, Let the earth put forth grass, herbs yielding seed, and fruit trees*

bearing fruit after their kind, wherein is the seed thereof, upon the earth: and it was so. And the earth brought forth grass, herbs yielding seed after their kind, and trees bearing fruit, wherein is the seed thereof, after their kind: and God saw that it was good.

Science also agrees with this account. After the formation of the Earth, rain fell upon the surface of the planet for millions of years. Eventually, all this water became the Earth's seas and oceans. The rain washed the minerals from the mountains and volcanoes into the seas, the cradle of animate life. Before vegetation, the Earth's atmosphere contained water, ammonia, carbon dioxide and other gases. There was no free oxygen. The free oxygen in the atmosphere was produced as the developing plant life took in carbon dioxide and released oxygen as a waste product.

In the *Genesis* account, the formation of the Earth's atmosphere is described as having taken place on the fourth day of creation.

And God said, Let there be lights in the firmament of heaven to divide the day from the night; and let them be for signs, and for seasons, and for days and years; and let them be for lights in the firmament of heaven to give light upon the earth: and it was so. And God made the two great lights; the greater light to rule the day, and the lesser light to rule the night: he made the stars also. And God set them in the firmament of heaven to give light upon the earth, and to rule over the day and over the night, and to divide the light from the darkness: and God saw that it was good.

Science also agrees with these statements. The Earth's early atmosphere was composed of heavy gases such as carbon dioxide, ammonia and sulfur dioxide. For millions of years, the light of the sun and stars, and the reflected light of the moon, could not penetrate this thick atmosphere.

Genesis describes the development of animal life on the fifth day of creation.

> *And God said, Let the waters swarm with swarms of living creatures, and let birds fly above the earth in the open firmament of heaven. And God created the great sea monsters, and every living creature that moveth, wherewith the waters swarmed, after their kind, and every winged bird after its kind; and God saw that it was good. And God blessed them, saying, Be fruitful, and multiply, and fill the waters in the seas, and let birds multiply on the earth.*

Science states that all animal life started in the seas and oceans. It was only after millions of years, and after millions of generations of simple life forms, that these primitive animals crawled out of the seas, onto dry land.

On the sixth day, *Genesis* describes the development of animal life on land, from the lower forms to man.

> *And God said, Let the earth bring forth living creatures after their kind, cattle, and creeping things, and beasts of the earth after their kind: and it was so. And God made the beasts of the earth after their kind, and the cattle after their kind, and everything that creepeth upon the ground after its kind: and God saw that it was good. And God said, Let us make man in our image, after our likeness:*

> *and let them have dominion over the fish of the sea, and over the birds of the heavens, and over the cattle, and over all the earth, and over every creeping thing that creepeth upon the earth. And God created man in his own image, in the image of God created he him: male and female created he them*

Science is in complete agreement with this entire sequence of creation as described in *the Book of Genesis.* The only difference comes about because of the differing interpretations of the amount of time involved. Science states that the beginning of creation occurred approximately fifteen billion years ago, and that there were eons between different phases of the universe's development. For instance, the sun and the planets in our solar system were formed approximately five billion years ago, the first single cells developed about four billion years ago, and only very recently did man appear upon the scene.

The Bible also describes definite stages of time during creation. However, the Bible describes these stages as being successive days, instead of long, successive periods of time as described by science. Many individuals have interpreted a *day* in the Bible to mean a twenty-four hour period. Science has strong evidence that a *day,* as described in the creation story of *Genesis,* must have been a very long period of time. Even in the Bible, it states that a day in eternity is as a thousand years. A *day* in the Bible must then be interpreted as a long and variable period of time.

Reviewing the two major authorities on the subject of creation, one can see that it can be viewed from two different aspects. From the creationists' view, each created form has its own life and is separate and detached from other life.

Man, God's highest creation, is taught that he is, in essence, different in form and kind from God. According to science, all life is of the same essence, that of energy. Creation began with one singularity, one starting point which is called the Big Bang. From this starting point, all life proceeded and developed. Throughout time, man has accepted either the *one life* or the *many lives* aspect.

Of the followers of the six major religions practiced today, Christians, Muslims and Jews believe and accept the many lives aspect of life. They believe that man is separate from God. This aspect of life is referred to as the *many lives* view. Another aspect of life is referred to as the *one life* view. Hindus, Buddhists and Taoists view life from this aspect; God exists and there is nothing but God, and therefore, there is only one life.

Man is an observer of the environment through his senses. He develops self-consciousness as he classifies what he observes as to how it affects him. As a result, he separates himself not only from all creations before him, but also from his fellow man. With this awareness of individuality, he naturally looks upon life as though there are many separate lives; he has his life and others have their own lives. Looking at life from this perspective causes man to become involved and to identify *only* with other expressions of his kind. He does not see himself as being a part of the lower expressions of life such as the stars, the planets, the plants and animals.

However, man does identify himself as being part of the human race, but in the process, he becomes emotionally involved. This is especially true of those with whom he associates in his daily life. This includes family, business associates, his church affiliates and other organizational groups to which he may belong. As man relates with those he associates, he begins to look upon himself as being inferior to some and superior to others. For example, if he encounters one who appears to have a greater ability than he has, he feels inferior to that individual. On the other hand, if he meets someone who appears to have less ability than he has, he feels superior. In identifying and classifying, man separates himself from his fellow man and ultimately from the oneness of life.

Man becomes enslaved to those that he feels inferior to and, as a result, he places them above him and accepts them as an authority to some degree. Man judges and condemns his own actions in accordance with what he has been taught. He is influenced by his religion, by his family and by his society's conventions. He has made these institutions his authorities, and as a result, he has become enslaved to them. Man is constantly belittling himself. He accepts the idea that he is a sinner or a failure in life. He fails to realize, even from his own Bible, that he is made in the image and likeness of God; that he is a free moral agent and that he has dominion over the beast within.

All these limiting views are the result of his lack of understanding that all life is one. All the great spiritual teachers observed and recognized the misery and suffering of humanity on the physical, mental and spiritual level. They all sought the cause of human suffering. Each of them went off into the 'wilderness', searching for the answers to this mystery. They left their home environments and went off alone into their inner world to contemplate, to question and to try to find the answer to the great mystery of life. During their sojourns in the 'wilderness', they each had a mystical experience in which they were given explicit instructions.

Something took over them while they were in this wilderness! A revelation came to these spiritual teachers. Once they returned to their normal environment, they began teaching that there was only one God. They taught that man could free himself from within and return to the Garden of Eden, the paradise lost. There are passages throughout the Bible, as well as in all sacred texts, which give accounts of the one life: "For in him we live, and move, and have our being"; "Ye are all sons of God in the making"; and "Hear Oh Israel, the Lord thy God is one".

It was claimed and stated by these great teachers that only a few would understand what they were teaching. To help the masses understand the meaning of life, they presented their teachings in an exoteric manner, in parables. Hidden within these exoteric stories were esoteric meanings. Concerning these hidden meanings, Jesus said, "He that hath an ear, let him hear". In other words, Jesus must have meant that it was possible to perceive through the superficial meaning and perceive the true, higher meaning behind the words.

In order to gain a greater understanding and perceive the esoteric meaning of the Scriptures, one must accept that there is only one life, one essence. This one life that expresses through man's form is not his own personal life. When one accepts that there is only one life, he then can retrace his steps on the road of life and take himself back to the paradise he once lost.

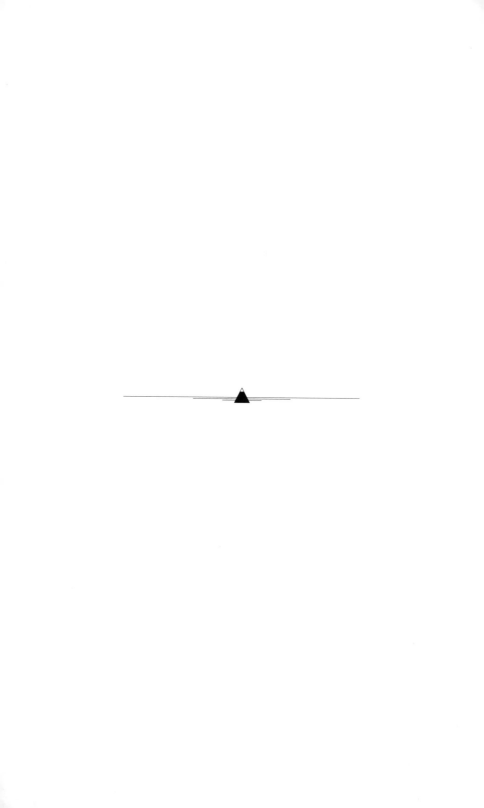

A New Beginning

Do you still have questions? Do you have a need to know more? If you have read this book and feel that there is a greater consciousness to achieve, a more abundant life to live, and that there exists ultimate freedom from enslavement, we offer to you **Life Engineering**, a course of instruction.

The instruction gives to its students the necessary tools to correlate science and theology. Using modern, scientific principles and the one life philosophy, Life Engineering reveals the scientific reality of oneness. It consists of three separate courses of instruction. The objective of the first course is to raise the student from the *self-conscious* level to the level of *rational consciousness*. Life Engineering has been taught throughout the United States and Canada for the past twenty years. **The Life Engineering Foundation** is a non-profit, scientific, educational organization that teaches the Life Engineering course of instruction.

For more information, please visit our Web site, contact our international headquarters or contact a Life Engineering center near you:

INTERNATIONAL

The Life Engineering Foundation
International Headquarters, **EOWATA**
2953 Delta Avenue
Bridgewater, Iowa
USA 50837-8015

Toll free: (800) 852-5072 (U.S. and Canada)
Phone: (515) 369-2391 (International)
Fax: (515) 369-4961
E-mail: office@lifeengineering.org
Web Site: **www.lifeengineering.org**

U.S. CENTERS

Omaha, Nebraska:
Contact Person: Beverly Thompson
3013 - S. 138 Street
Omaha, Nebraska
USA 68144
Phone: (402) 334-5334

Las Vegas, Nevada:
Contact Person: Harold Ford
#577, 6666 - W Washington Avenue
Las Vegas, Nevada
USA 89107
Phone: (702) 258-9435

Anacortes, Washington:
Contact Person: Jack Newton
4212 - Glasgow Way
Anacortes, Washington
USA 98221
Phone: (360) 293-5057

CANADIAN CENTERS

Calgary, Alberta:
Canadian Headquarters
Contact Person: Dr. Ron Armstrong
2457 - 22A Street NW
Calgary, Alberta
Canada T2M 3X8
Phone: (403) 282-1011

Edmonton, Alberta:
Contact Person: Terry Curtis
#8, 3115 - 119 Street
Edmonton, Alberta
Canada T6J 5N5
Phone: (780) 988-8980

Montreal, Quebec:
Contact Person: Dr. Jacques Bernard
#101, 260 - Taggart
Greenfield Park, Quebec
Canada J4V 2Y5
Phone: (450) 923-8913